BANJO FRETBOARD ATLAS

GET A BETTER GRIP ON NECK NAVIGATION!

BY JOE CHARUPAKORN

ISBN 978-1-4950-8039-5

Visit Hal Leonard Online at
www.halleonard.com

Contact Us:
Hal Leonard
7777 West Bluemound Road
Milwaukee, WI 53213
Email: info@halleonard.com

In Europe contact:
Hal Leonard Europe Limited
Distribution Centre, Newmarket Road
Bury St Edmunds, Suffolk, IP33 3YB
Email: info@halleonardeurope.com

In Australia contact:
Hal Leonard Australia Pty. Ltd.
4 Lentara Court
Cheltenham, Victoria, 3192 Australia
Email: info@halleonard.com.au

TABLE OF CONTENTS

INTRODUCTION

Banjo Fretboard Atlas is a collection of roadmaps for the most important scales and chords (up to seventh chords) in standard G tuning. The material is presented in all 12 keys, using 12-fret neck diagrams with color-coded displays of the most common moveable fingerings. When fingerings share common notes, the colors will overlap. No music reading or understanding of music theory is required.

Mastering the 5-string banjo neck can be challenging, even for very experienced players. There are several obstacles that make learning the banjo's fretboard difficult. On the banjo, a note can be played in several different places, unlike many other instruments, where each note has only one location.

The diagrams in *Banjo Fretboard Atlas* will help you quickly internalize and memorize not only the most common scales and chords, but also others that may have previously seemed impossible to grasp. You'll be able to easily see and understand how scale and chord shapes are laid out and how they connect and overlap across the neck. As an added benefit, once you can see a shape in your mind's eye, you've got all 12 keys covered—just move the shape to start on a different fret, depending on the key you want.

ABOUT THE AUTHOR

New York City native Joe Charupakorn is a guitarist, editor, and best-selling author. He has written over 25 instructional books for Hal Leonard. His books are available worldwide and have been translated into many languages.

Visit him on the web at joecharupakorn.com.

HOW TO USE THIS BOOK

A good plan of attack with *Banjo Fretboard Atlas* would be to start by learning the most common scales, which are the major, natural minor (Aeolian), minor pentatonic, major pentatonic, and blues scales. After getting comfortable with these (or if and when the need arises), then add in some of the more complex scales and modes presented in this book.

First, start with one scale shape and work with it for a while in one key until it feels comfortable. When you've internalized that one shape, add in an adjacent shape in the same key. Once you can see both shapes independently and also as pieces of a bigger puzzle, then practice going back and forth between the two. Eventually add in more fingerings in the same key; before long, you'll have the whole neck covered. There are countless ways to put the scale shapes to use. For example, you can run the scales straight up and down, improvise with them, or sight-read, using the shapes as a reference. Do this in all 12 keys.

For the chord section, start with power chords and triads, which are the backbone of virtually any style of music and fall into the "must-know" category. After you've got a firm grasp on these chords, learn the triads with added notes and seventh chords to add harmonic color to your music. To internalize chord shapes, first take some time to get a mental picture of the chord's shape. After committing it to memory, practice getting to the shape quickly without referring to the book, and also make sure all the notes are ringing clearly. Then add another voicing of the same chord and practice moving back and forth between the two voicings. Once you are comfortable with this, do it in the remaining keys. To gain flexibility with the new chords, practice a short progression of two or three chords in different keys, at first using two voicings for each chord. Then add more voicings as it becomes second nature. Also try creating solo arrangements of some of your favorite tunes and put these new shapes to use.

Beyond the Fingering

For each diagram, every tone of the specific scale or chord is circled, but only the most common moveable shapes are displayed with color codes. Note that, because the banjo's fifth string is most commonly used as a drone and rarely fretted, the fingerings in this book are only color coded from the fourth to the first strings.

The fingerings presented are just a starting point—you shouldn't feel "locked in" to any of the shapes presented. Feel free to experiment! You can take fragments from one fingering and combine it with fragments from an adjacent fingering to create your own shapes that might be more suitable for a specific situation. Use the circled scale and chord tones as a guide and go for it! Because they all interconnect, the idea is that, ultimately, you'll see the banjo neck as one unit.

NOTATION CONVENTIONS IN THIS BOOK

Any note with an *accidental*—a sharp or flat—can be spelled either as a sharp or flat version of the note. In this book, both the sharp and flat versions of every note (*enharmonic equivalents*) are displayed on the fretboard diagrams. The specific accidentals used in the "proper" spelling of a scale or chord will generally depend on the context.

For example, here is the proper spelling of the G major scale:

G A B C D E F♯ G

And here is an incorrect spelling of the G major scale:

G A B C D E G♭ G

F♯ is the same note as G♭, and, in our diagrams, any note location with that pitch is represented by F♯/G♭ on the fretboard. However, the correct spelling of the G major scale is the one with F♯ because this spelling lets us represent every letter in the music alphabet. In the spelling with G♭, there are no Fs of any kind and two kinds of Gs—a G♭ and a G.

In the headings above the diagrams throughout the book, only the most commonly accepted spellings of the specific scales or chords are displayed.

Exceptions to the Rule

In some cases, it's more practical to suspend the rigidity of the rules and go with a more familiar, if technically "wrong," spelling. This is particularly common in cases involving scales and chords that have double sharps (𝄪) and double flats (𝄫) in their proper spelling.

The fretboard diagrams in *Banjo Fretboard Atlas* do not include double sharps (𝄪) or double flats (𝄫), or less common accidentals such as F♭, C♭, etc. However, the proper spellings of scales and chords are listed in the headings above the diagrams throughout the book.

For example, the proper spelling of A♭ melodic minor is:

A♭ B♭ C♭ D♭ E♭ F♭ G

While F♭ is enharmonically the same note as E, the dots representing the F♭ notes will be on the fretboard diagram's E notes. Likewise, while C♭ is enharmonically the same note as B, the dots representing the C♭ notes will be on the fretboard diagram's B notes.

If this is all a little confusing, the good news is that, even without any of this information, you'll be able to play any of the scales or chords in any key as long as you can follow the diagrams.

All the chords diagramed in this book consist of two, three and four notes. Usually six-nine and minor six-nine chords contain five notes, but since we've been fretting the notes on strings one through four, we need to omit a note from these five-note chords. The note that is traditionally eliminated in this circumstance is the fifth of the chord. The remaining notes (1–3–6–9) are all that's needed to capture the essence of the harmony.

Some of the fingerings of the four-note chords require a wide stretch, particularly the ones down near the first fret. Remember that these shapes can be played above the twelfth fret, making them much more comfortable to play.

SCALES

THE MAJOR SCALE AND ITS MODES

C IONIAN

C–D–E–F–G–A–B

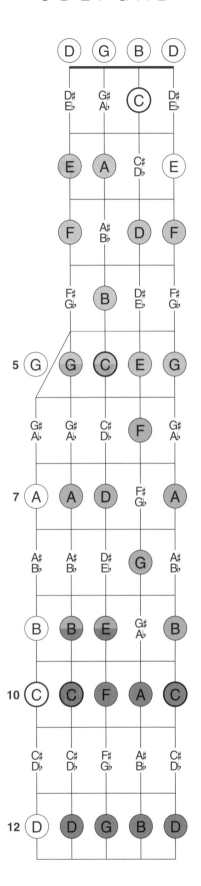

C#/D♭ IONIAN

C#–D#–E#–F#–G#–A#–B#
D♭–E♭–F–G♭–A♭–B♭–C

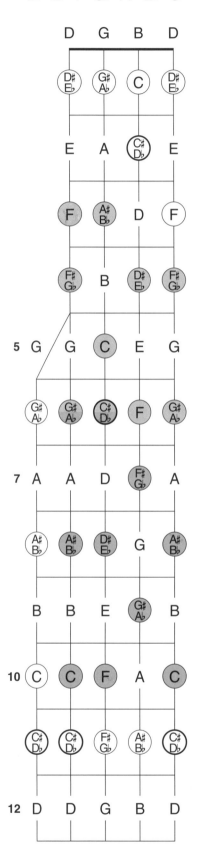

D IONIAN

D–E–F#–G–A–B–C#

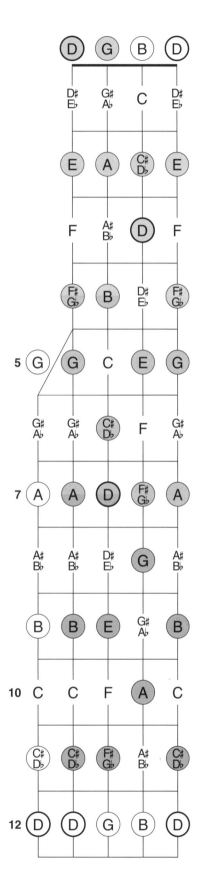

E♭ IONIAN

E♭–F–G–A♭–B♭–C–D

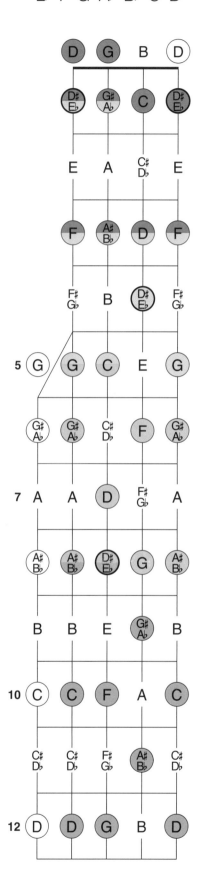

E IONIAN

E–F#–G#–A–B–C#–D#

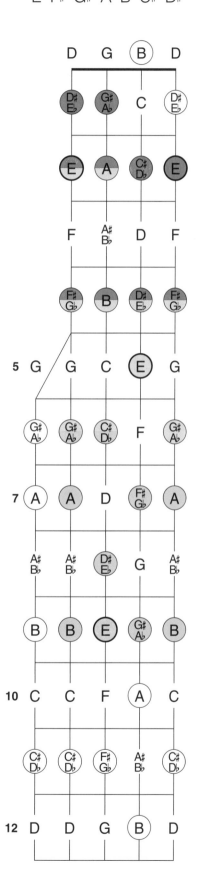

F IONIAN

F–G–A–B♭–C–D–E

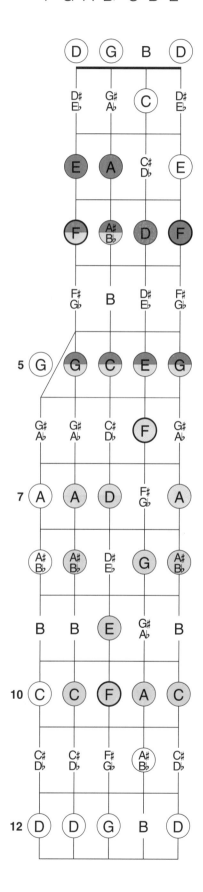

F#/G♭ IONIAN

F#–G#–A#–B–C#–D#–E#
G♭–A♭–B♭–C♭–D♭–E♭–F

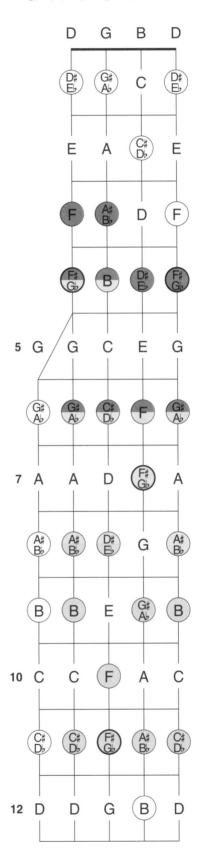

G IONIAN

G–A–B–C–D–E–F#

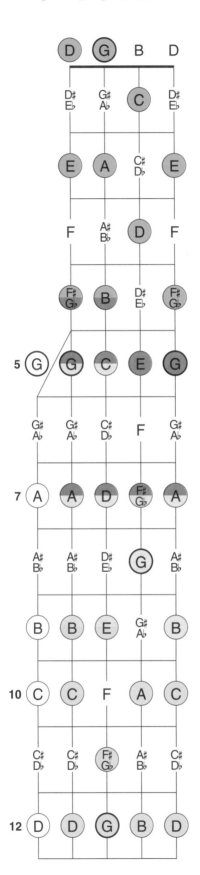

A♭ IONIAN

A♭–B♭–C–D♭–E♭–F–G

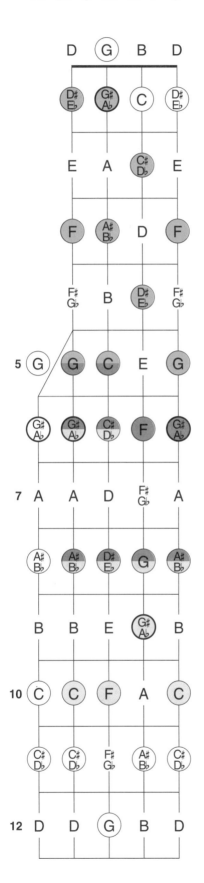

A IONIAN

A–B–C#–D–E–F#–G#

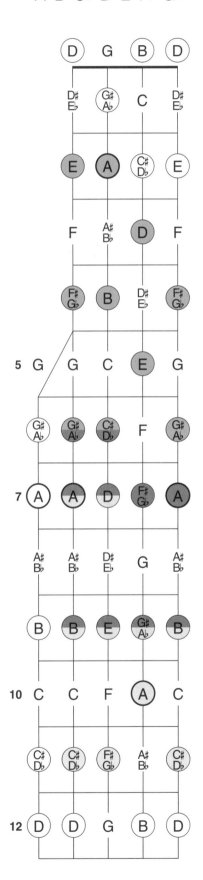

B♭ IONIAN

B♭–C–D–E♭–F–G–A

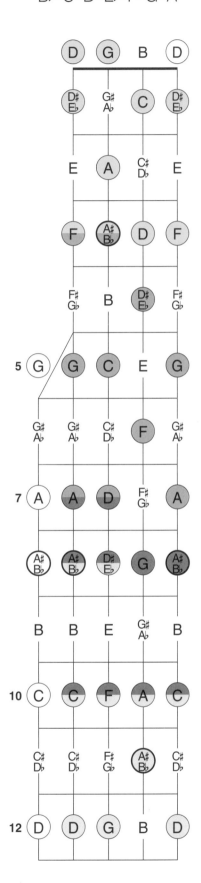

B IONIAN

B–C#–D#–E–F#–G#–A#

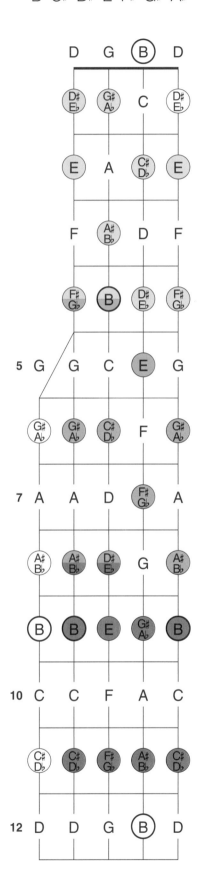

C DORIAN

C–D–E♭–F–G–A–B♭

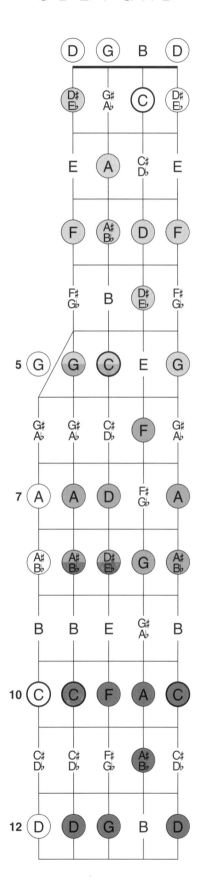

C♯ DORIAN

C♯–D♯–E–F♯–G♯–A♯–B

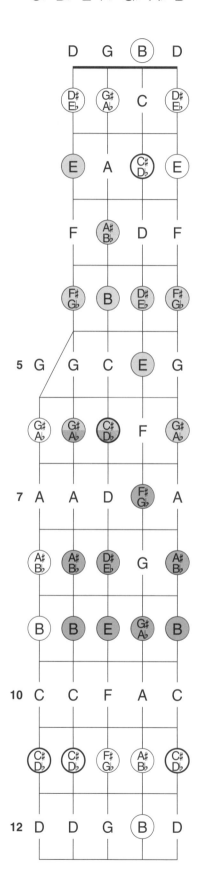

D DORIAN

D–E–F–G–A–B–C

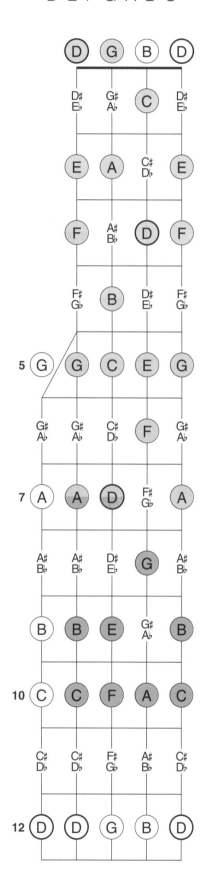

Eb DORIAN

Eb–F–Gb–Ab–Bb–C–Db

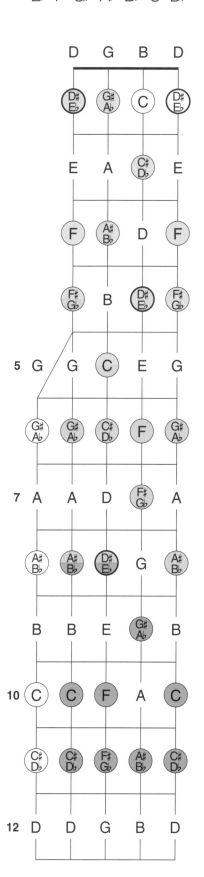

E DORIAN

E–F#–G–A–B–C#–D

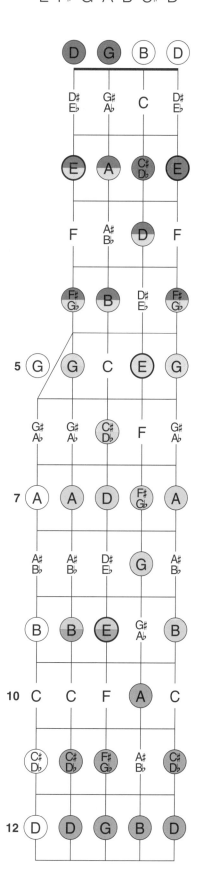

F DORIAN

F–G–Ab–Bb–C–D–Eb

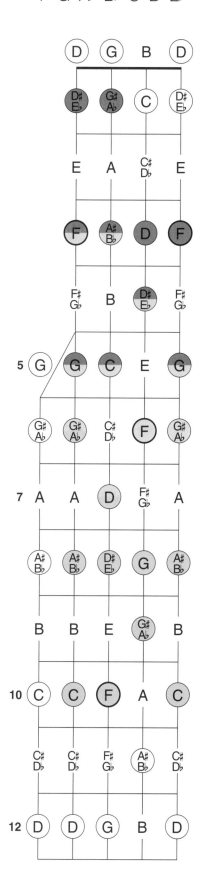

F# DORIAN

F#–G#–A–B–C#–D#–E

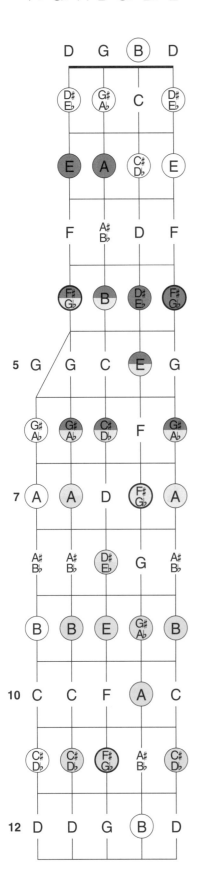

G DORIAN

G–A–Bb–C–D–E–F

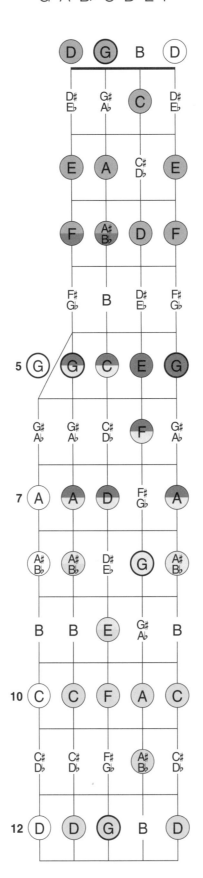

Ab DORIAN

Ab–Bb–Cb–Db–Eb–F–Gb

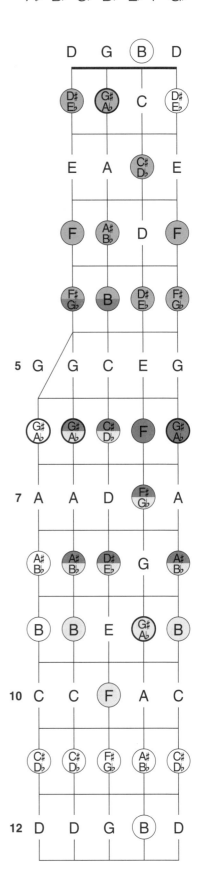

A DORIAN

A–B–C–D–E–F#–G

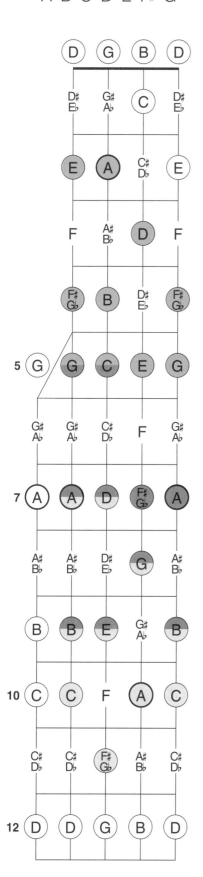

Bb DORIAN

Bb–C–Db–Eb–F–G–Ab

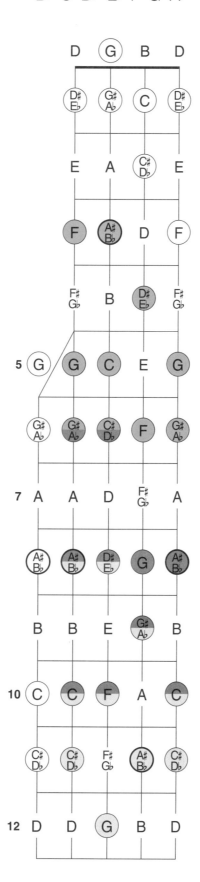

B DORIAN

B–C#–D–E–F#–G#–A

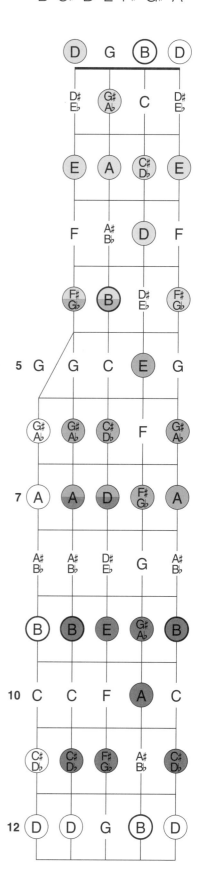

C PHRYGIAN

C–Db–Eb–F–G–Ab–Bb

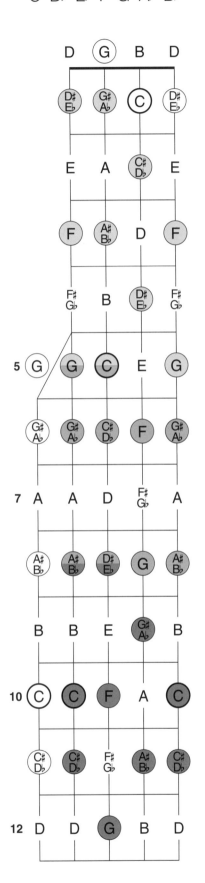

C# PHRYGIAN

C#–D–E–F#–G#–A–B

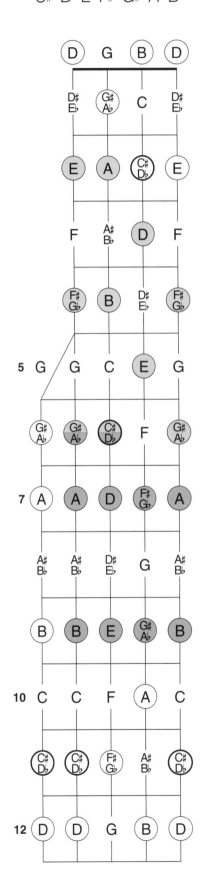

D PHRYGIAN

D–Eb–F–G–A–Bb–C

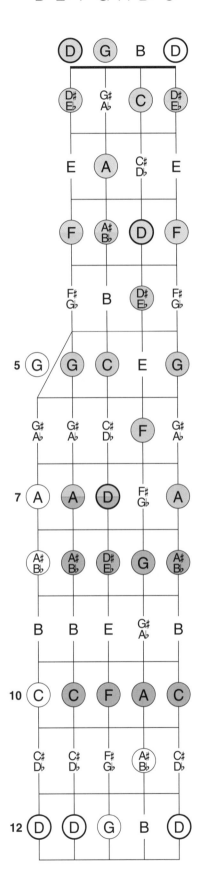

D♯ PHRYGIAN

D♯–E–F♯–G♯–A♯–B–C♯

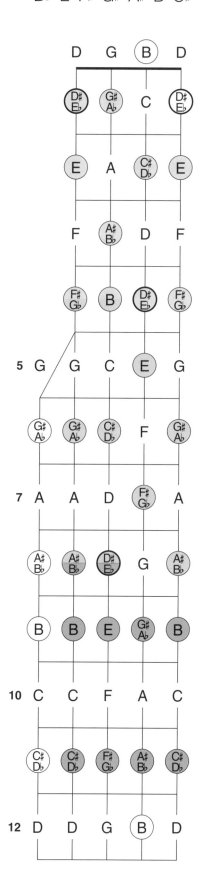

E PHRYGIAN

E–F–G–A–B–C–D

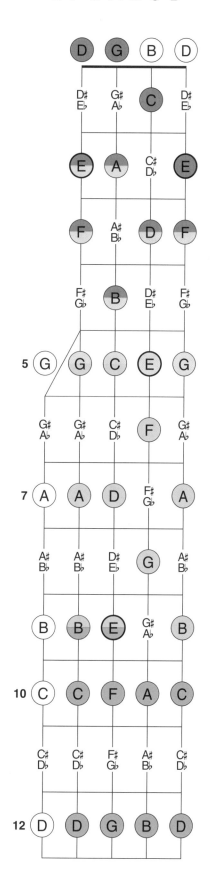

F PHRYGIAN

F–G♭–A♭–B♭–C–D♭–E♭

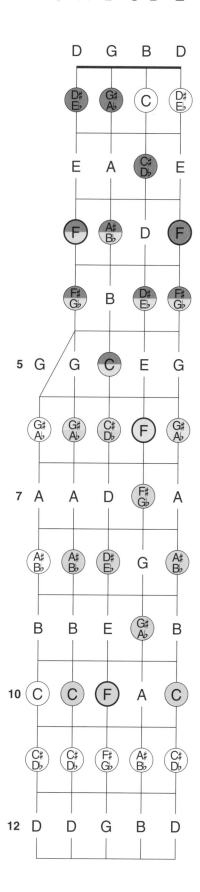

F# PHRYGIAN

F#–G–A–B–C#–D–E

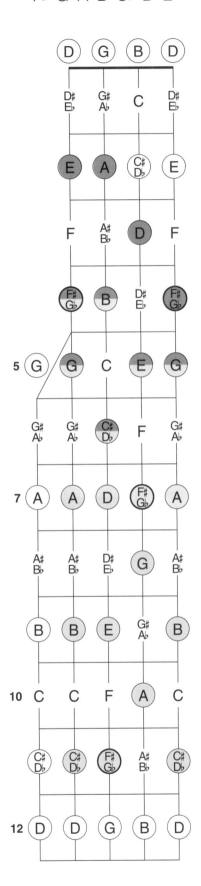

G PHRYGIAN

G–A♭–B♭–C–D–E♭–F

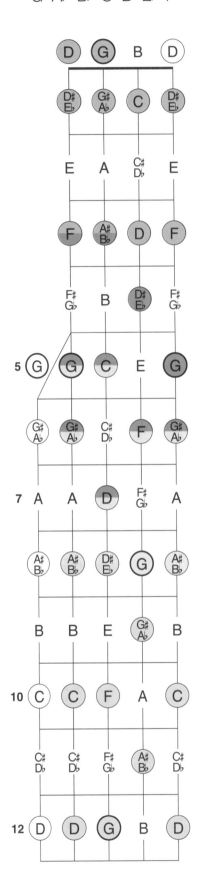

G# PHRYGIAN

G#–A–B–C#–D#–E–F#

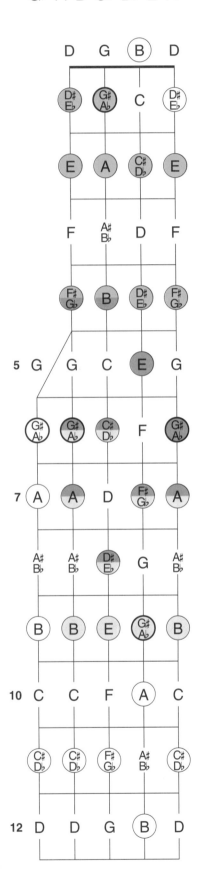

A PHRYGIAN

A–B♭–C–D–E–F–G

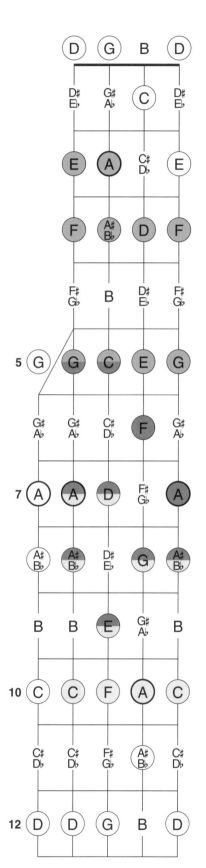

B♭ PHRYGIAN

B♭–C♭–D♭–E♭–F–G♭–A♭

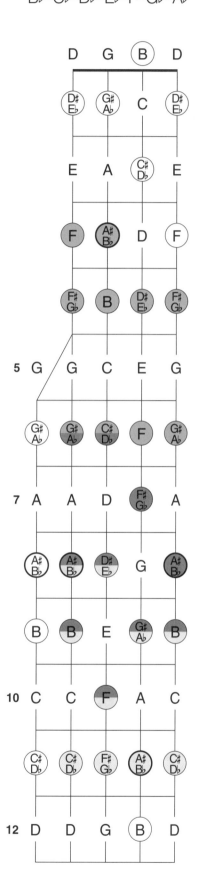

B PHRYGIAN

B–C–D–E–F♯–G–A

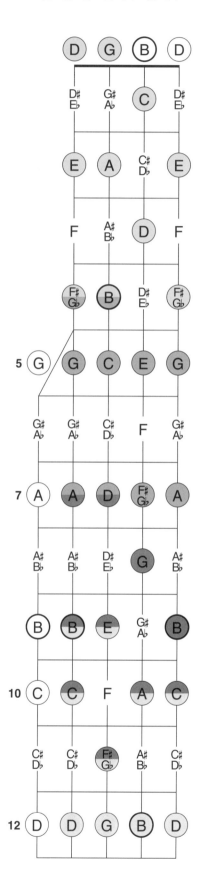

C LYDIAN

C–D–E–F#–G–A–B

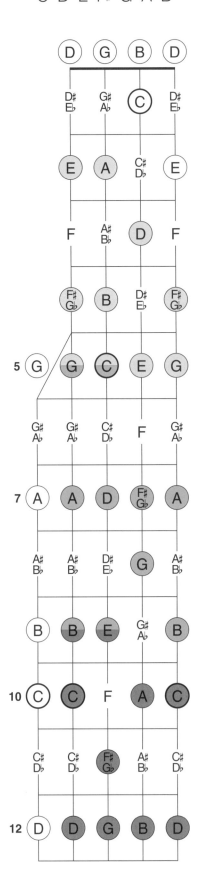

Db LYDIAN

Db–Eb–F–G–Ab–Bb–C

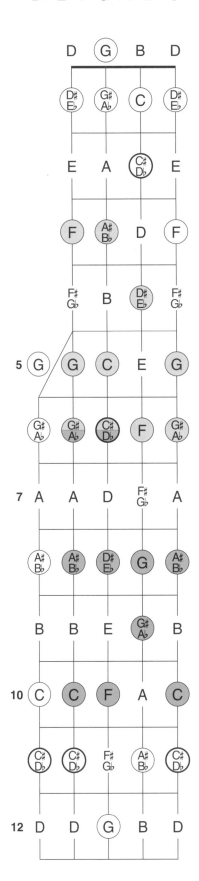

D LYDIAN

D–E–F#–G#–A–B–C#

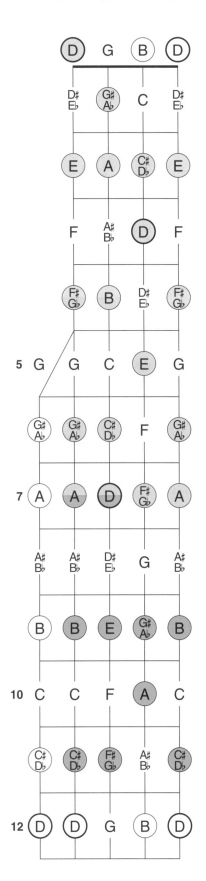

E♭ LYDIAN

E♭–F–G–A–B♭–C–D

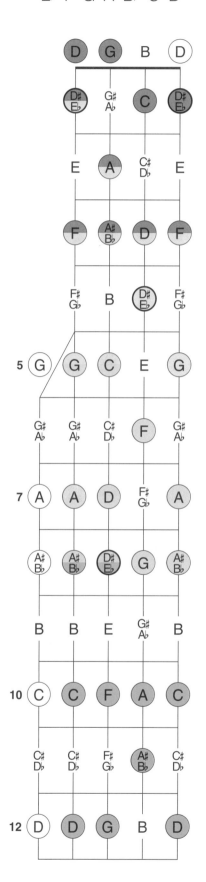

E LYDIAN

E–F#–G#–A#–B–C#–D#

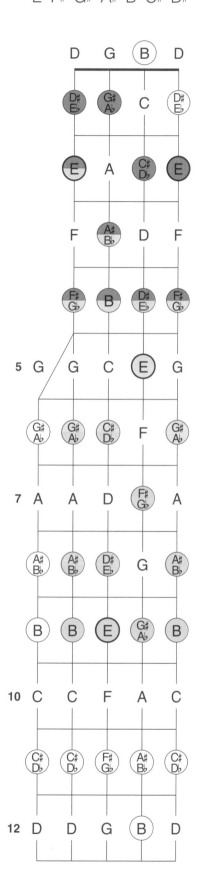

F LYDIAN

F–G–A–B–C–D–E

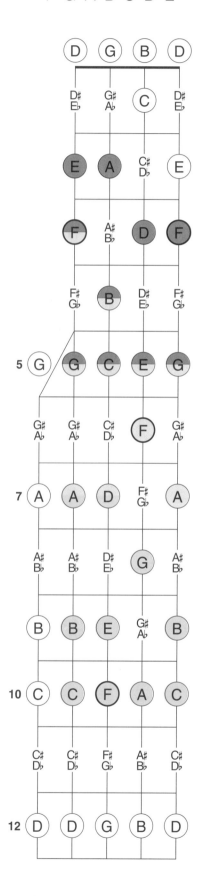

F#/Gb LYDIAN

F#–G#–A#–B#–C#–D#–E#
Gb–Ab–Bb–C–Db–Eb–F

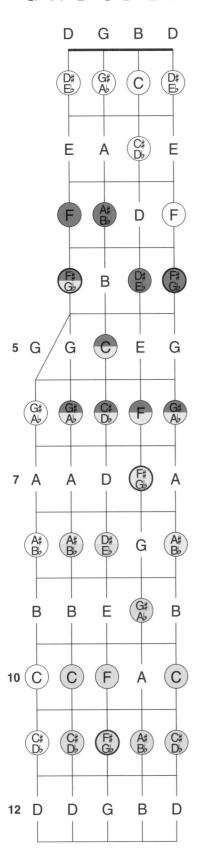

G LYDIAN

G–A–B–C#–D–E–F#

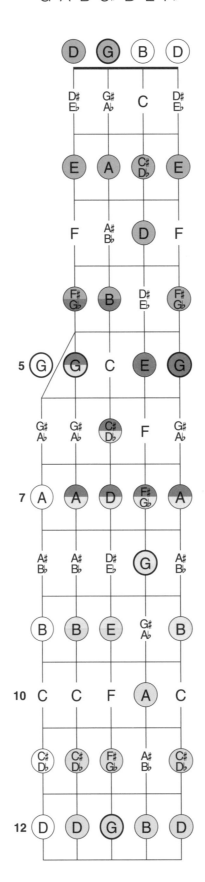

Ab LYDIAN

Ab–Bb–C–D–Eb–F–G

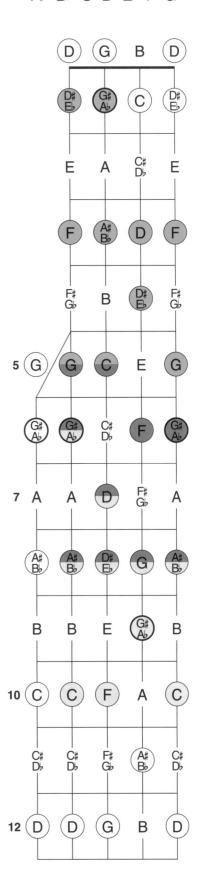

A LYDIAN

A–B–C#–D#–E–F#–G#

B♭ LYDIAN

B♭–C–D–E–F–G–A

B LYDIAN

B–C#–D#–E#–F#–G#–A#

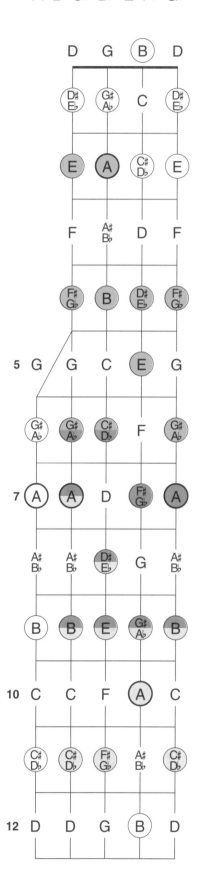

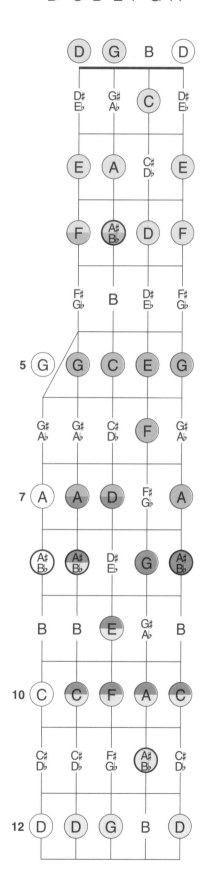

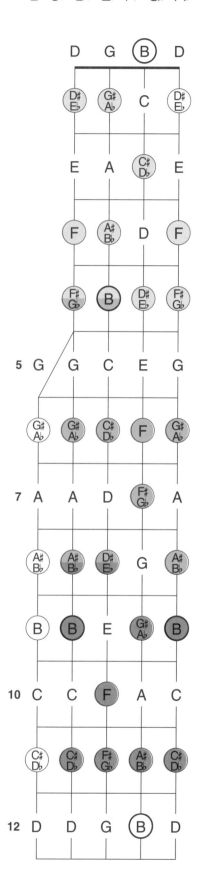

C MIXOLYDIAN

C–D–E–F–G–A–B♭

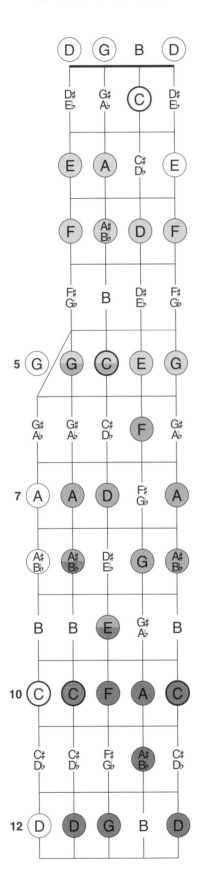

C♯/D♭ MIXOLYDIAN

C♯–D♯–E♯–F♯–G♯–A♯–B
D♭–E♭–F–G♭–A♭–B♭–C♭

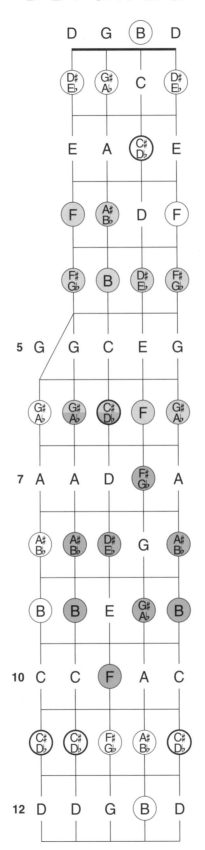

D MIXOLYDIAN

D–E–F♯–G–A–B–C

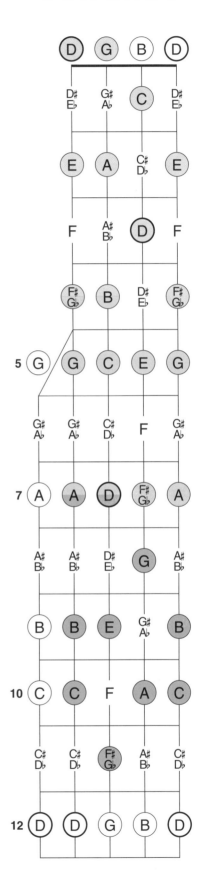

Eb MIXOLYDIAN

Eb–F–G–Ab–Bb–C–Db

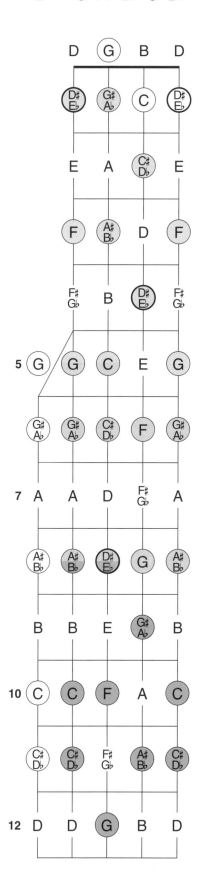

E MIXOLYDIAN

E–F#–G#–A–B–C#–D

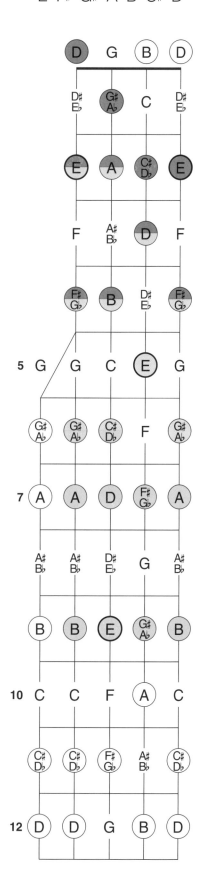

F MIXOLYDIAN

F–G–A–Bb–C–D–Eb

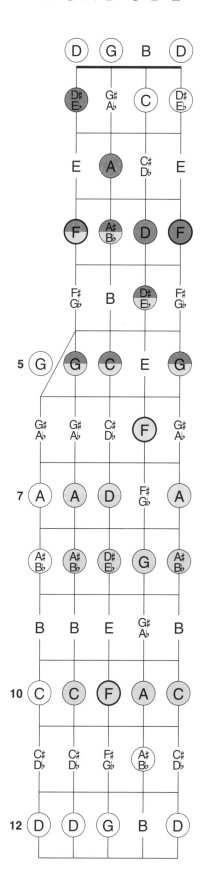

F♯/G♭ MIXOLYDIAN

F♯–G♯–A♯–B–C♯–D♯–E
G♭–A♭–B♭–C♭–D♭–E♭–F♭

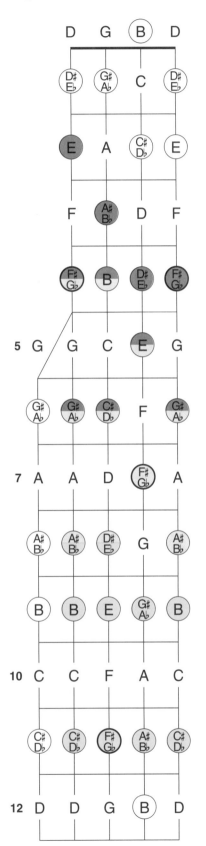

G MIXOLYDIAN

G–A–B–C–D–E–F

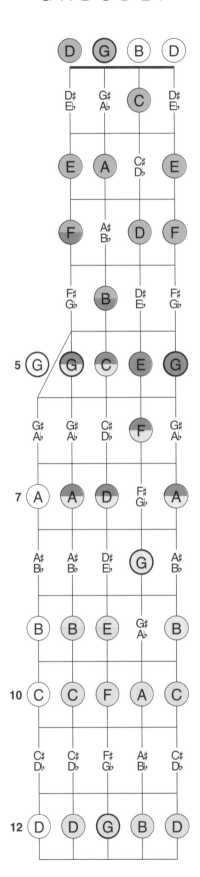

A♭ MIXOLYDIAN

A♭–B♭–C–D♭–E♭–F–G♭

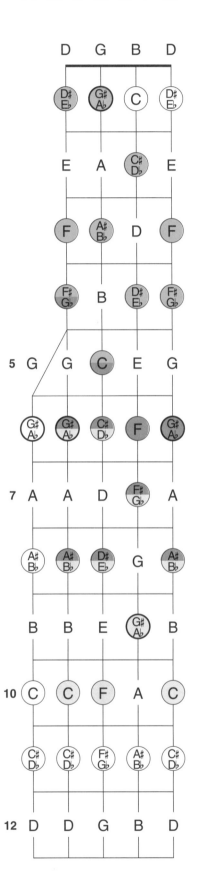

A MIXOLYDIAN

A–B–C#–D–E–F#–G

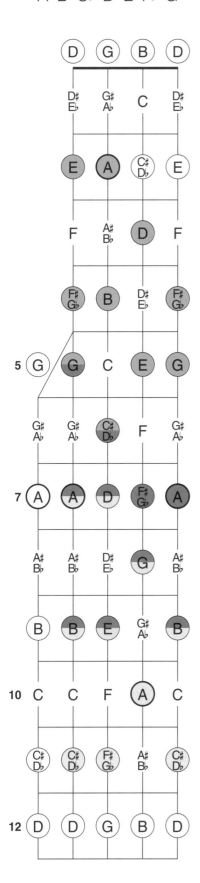

B♭ MIXOLYDIAN

B♭–C–D–E♭–F–G–A♭

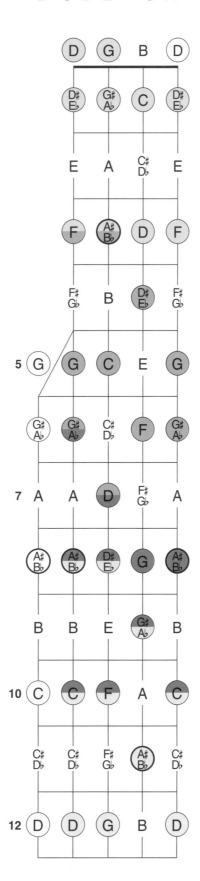

B MIXOLYDIAN

B–C#–D#–E–F#–G#–A

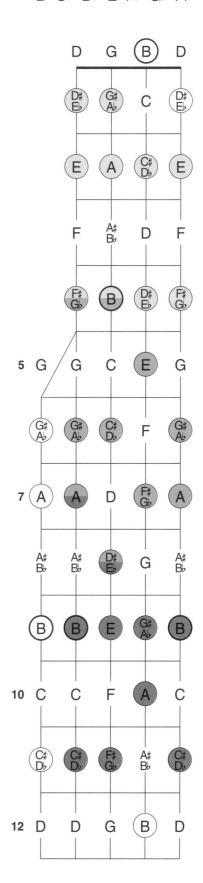

C AEOLIAN

C–D–E♭–F–G–A♭–B♭

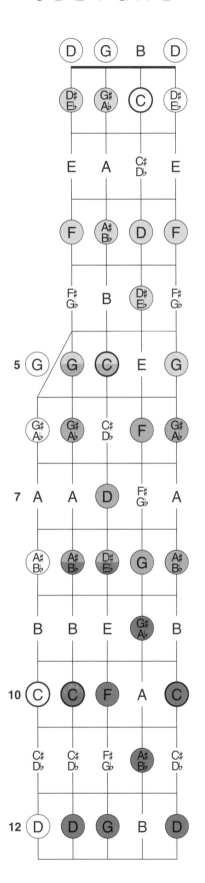

C♯ AEOLIAN

C♯–D♯–E–F♯–G♯–A–B

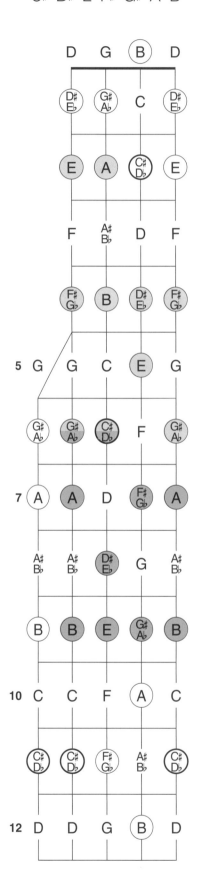

D AEOLIAN

D–E–F–G–A–B♭–C

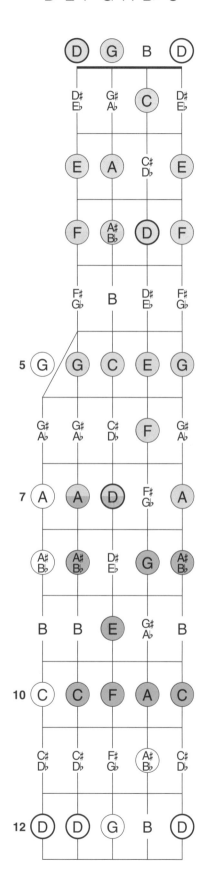

D#/Eb AEOLIAN

D#–E#–F#–G#–A#–B–C#
Eb–F–Gb–Ab–Bb–Cb–Db

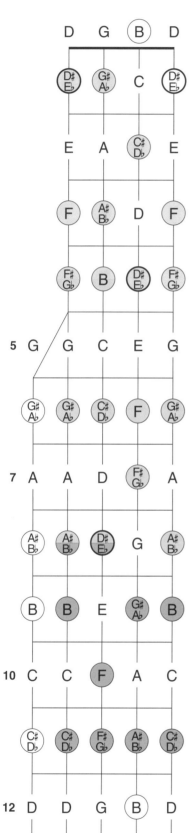

E AEOLIAN

E–F#–G–A–B–C–D

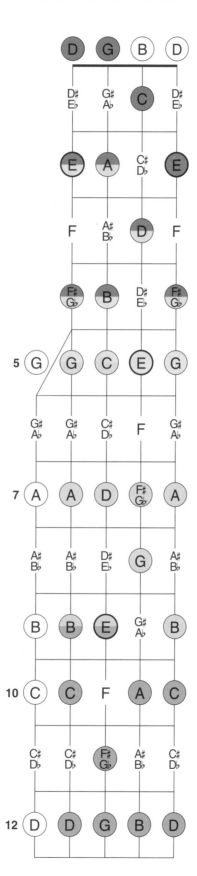

F AEOLIAN

F–G–Ab–Bb–C–Db–Eb

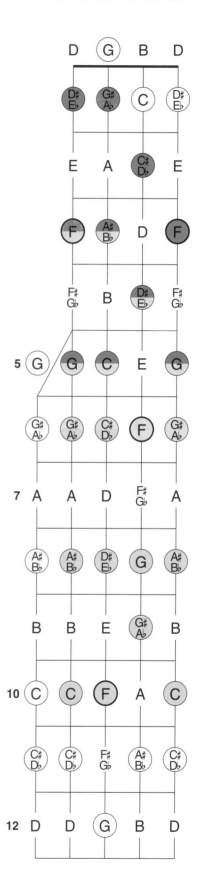

F# AEOLIAN

F#–G#–A–B–C#–D–E

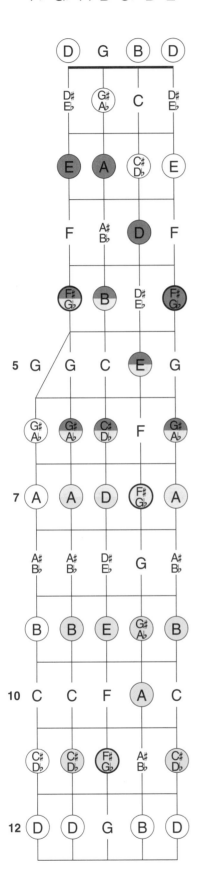

G AEOLIAN

G–A–B♭–C–D–E♭–F

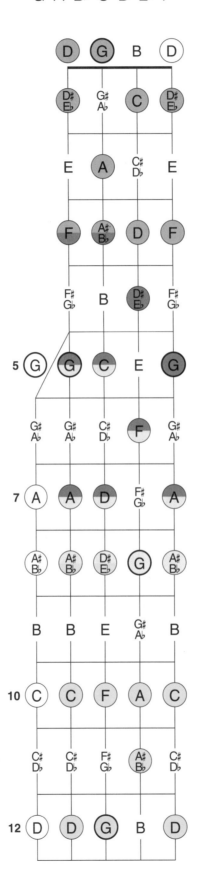

G#/A♭ AEOLIAN

G#–A#–B–C#–D#–E–F#
A♭–B♭–C♭–D♭–E♭–F♭–G♭

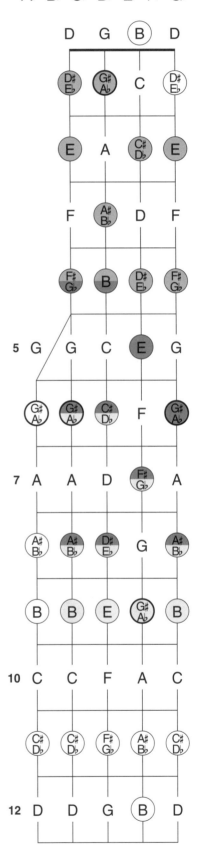

A AEOLIAN

A–B–C–D–E–F–G

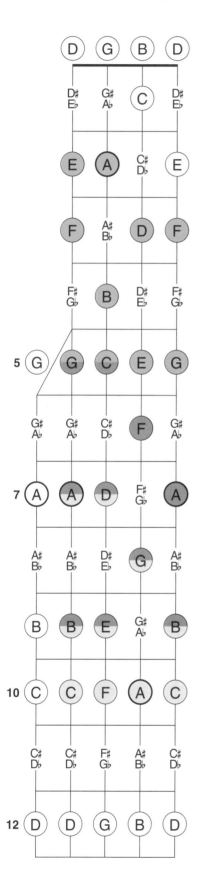

Bb AEOLIAN

Bb–C–Db–Eb–F–Gb–Ab

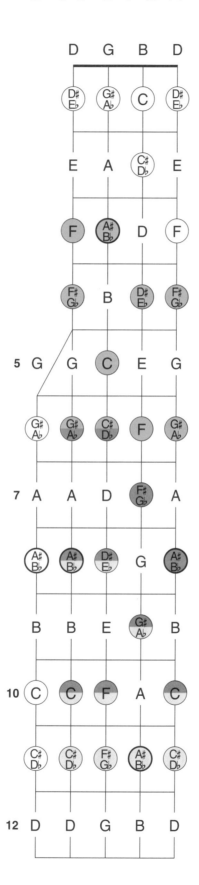

B AEOLIAN

B–C#–D–E–F#–G–A

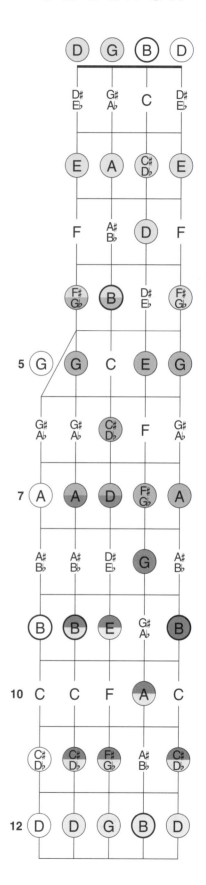

31

C LOCRIAN

C–Db–Eb–F–Gb–Ab–Bb

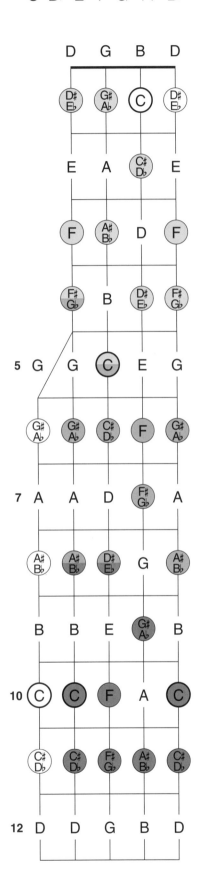

C# LOCRIAN

C#–D–E–F#–G–A–B

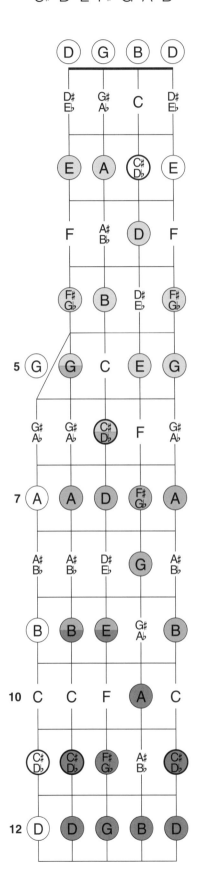

D LOCRIAN

D–Eb–F–G–Ab–Bb–C

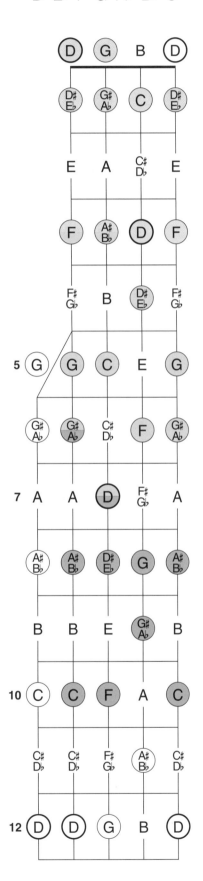

D♯ LOCRIAN

D♯–E–F♯–G♯–A–B–C♯

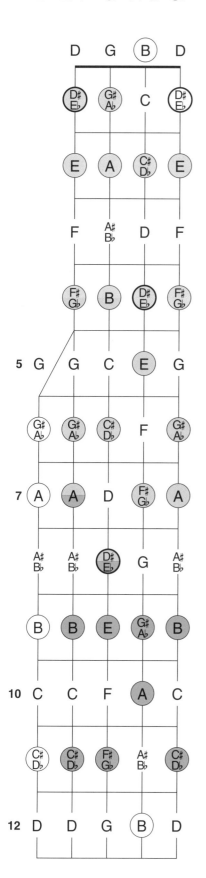

E LOCRIAN

E–F–G–A–B♭–C–D

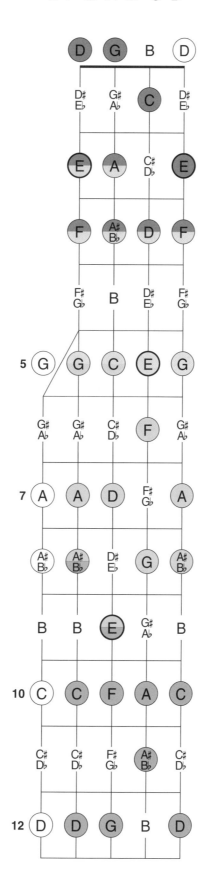

F LOCRIAN

F–G♭–A♭–B♭–C♭–D♭–E♭

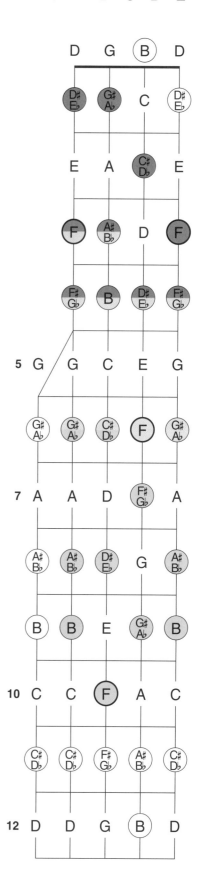

F# LOCRIAN

F#–G–A–B–C–D–E

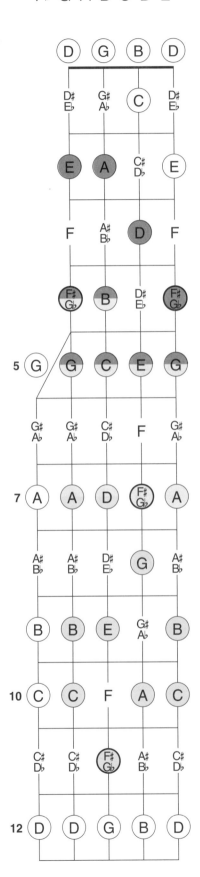

G LOCRIAN

G–Ab–Bb–C–Db–Eb–F

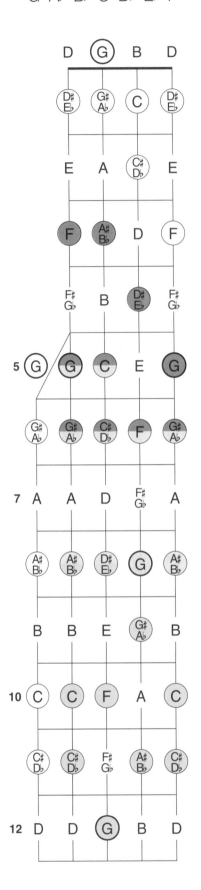

G# LOCRIAN

G#–A–B–C#–D–E–F#

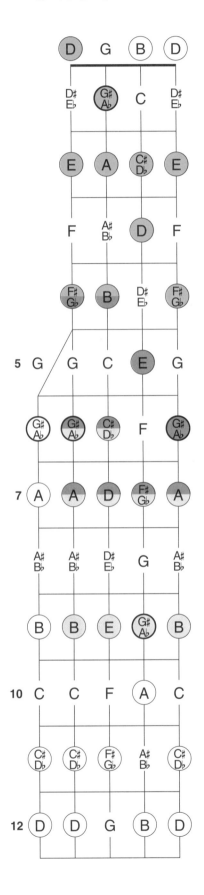

A LOCRIAN

A–B♭–C–D–E♭–F–G

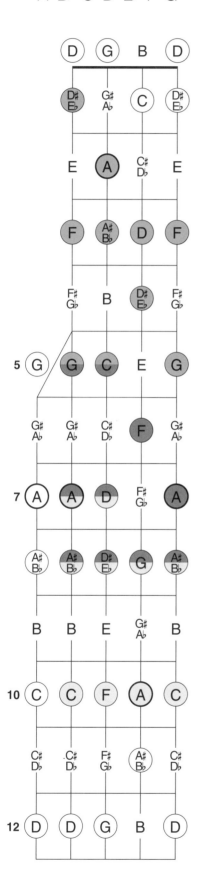

A♯ LOCRIAN

A♯–B–C♯–D♯–E–F♯–G♯

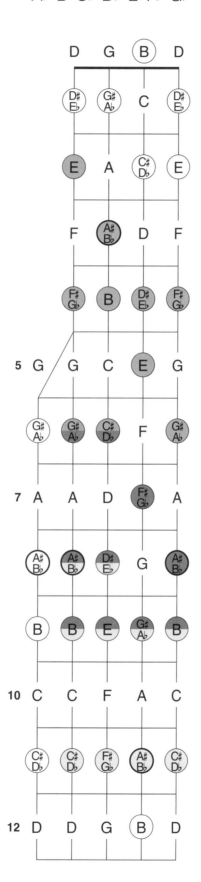

B LOCRIAN

B–C–D–E–F–G–A

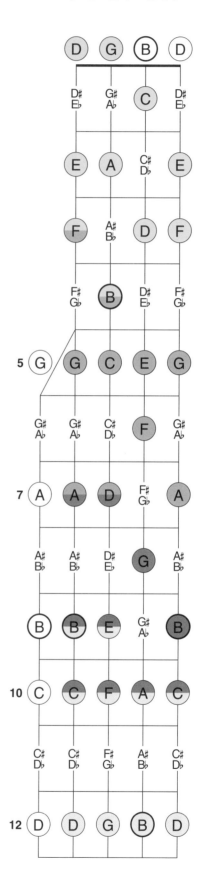

SCALES

PENTATONIC AND BLUES SCALES

C MAJOR PENTATONIC

C–D–E–G–A

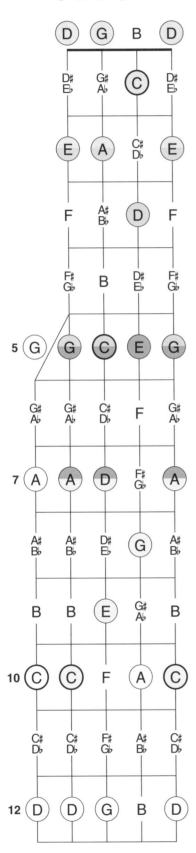

Db MAJOR PENTATONIC

Db–Eb–F–Ab–Bb

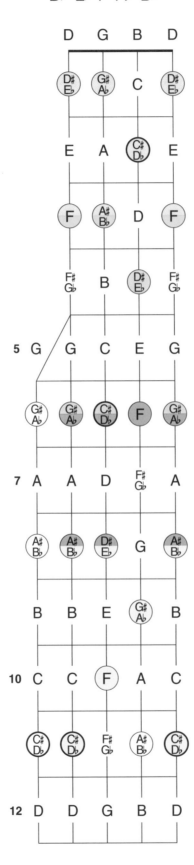

D MAJOR PENTATONIC

D–E–F#–A–B

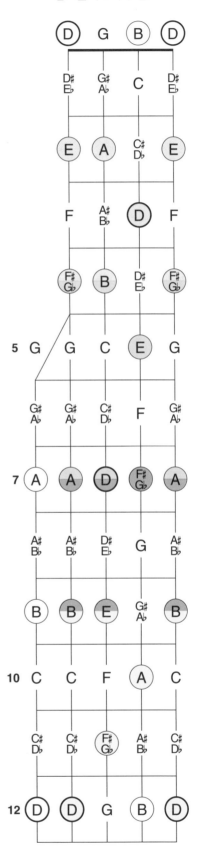

Eb MAJOR PENTATONIC

Eb–F–G–Bb–C

E MAJOR PENTATONIC

E–F#–G#–B–C#

F MAJOR PENTATONIC

F–G–A–C–D

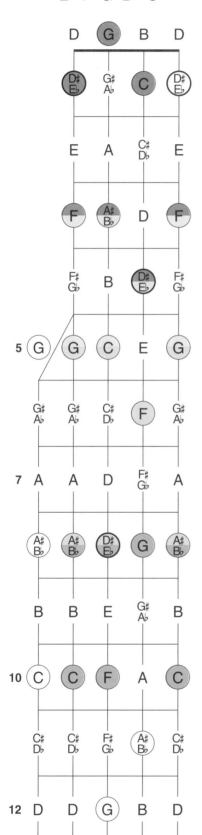

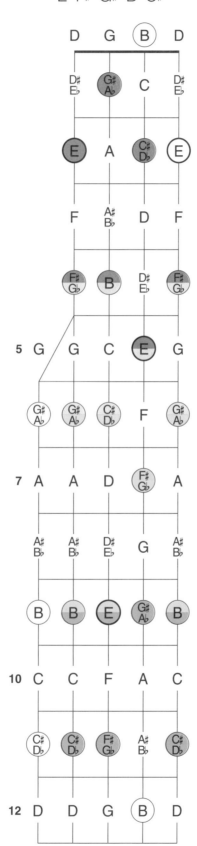

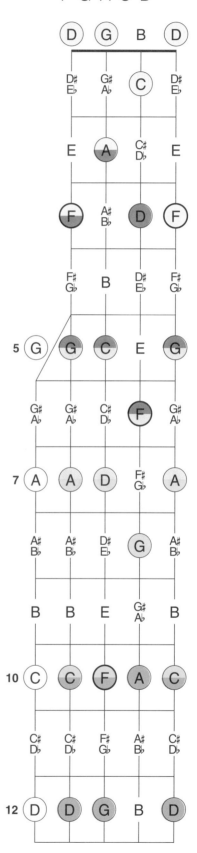

F#/Gb MAJOR PENTATONIC

F#–G#–A#–C#–D#
Gb–Ab–Bb–Db–Eb

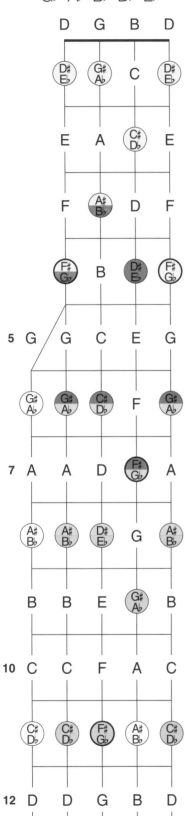

G MAJOR PENTATONIC

G–A–B–D–E

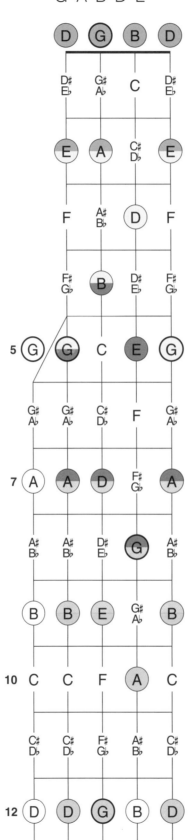

Ab MAJOR PENTATONIC

Ab–Bb–C–Eb–F

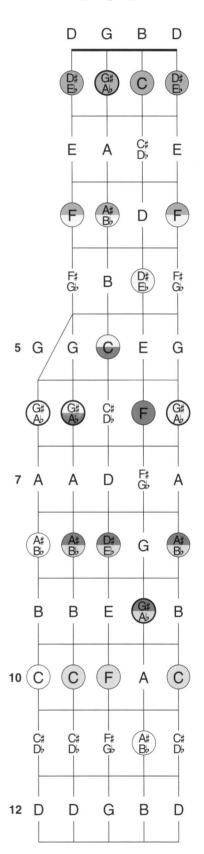

A MAJOR
PENTATONIC

A–B–C#–E–F#

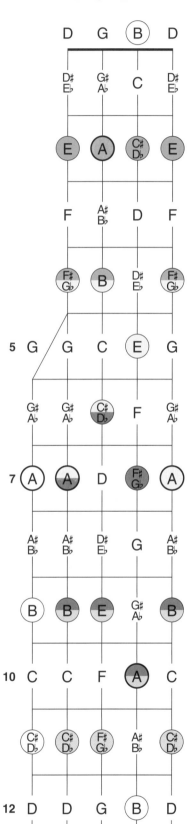

B♭ MAJOR
PENTATONIC

B♭–C–D–F–G

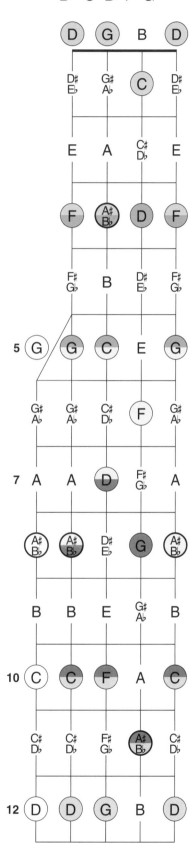

B MAJOR
PENTATONIC

B–C#–D#–F#–G#

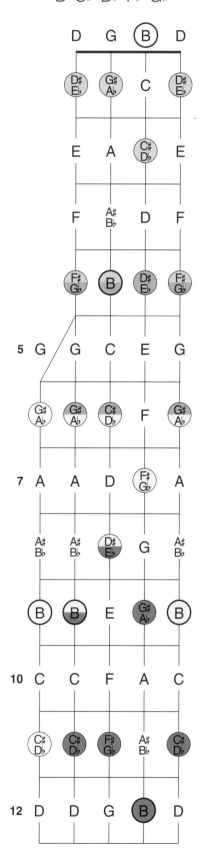

C MINOR PENTATONIC

C–Eb–F–G–Bb

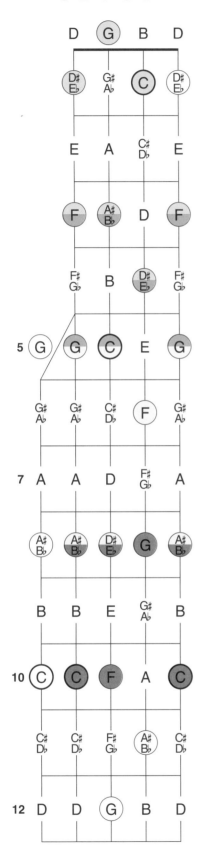

C# MINOR PENTATONIC

C#–E–F#–G#–B

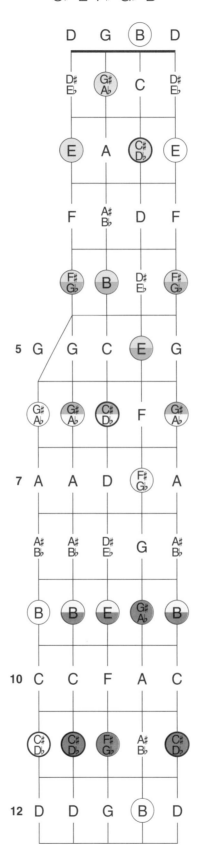

D MINOR PENTATONIC

D–F–G–A–C

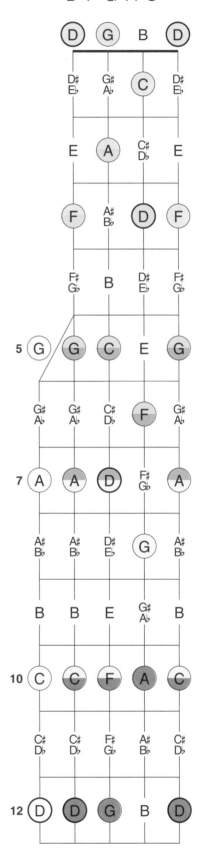

D#/E♭ MINOR PENTATONIC

D#–F#–G#–A#–C#
E♭–G♭–A♭–B♭–D♭

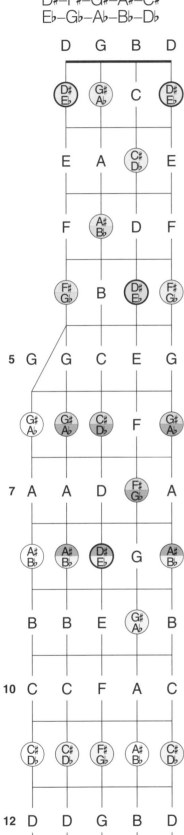

E MINOR PENTATONIC

E–G–A–B–D

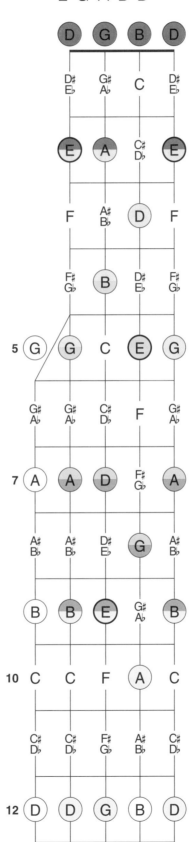

F MINOR PENTATONIC

F–A♭–B♭–C–E♭

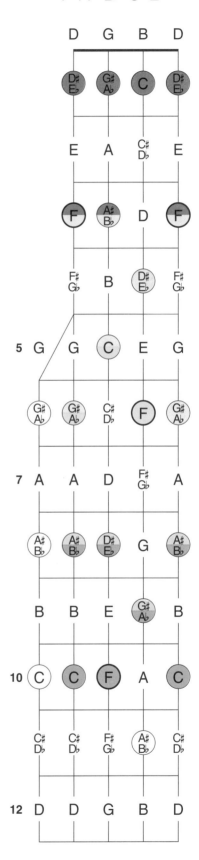

43

F♯ MINOR PENTATONIC

F♯–A–B–C♯–E

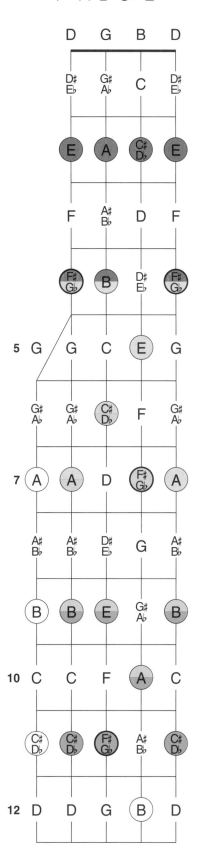

G MINOR PENTATONIC

G–B♭–C–D–F

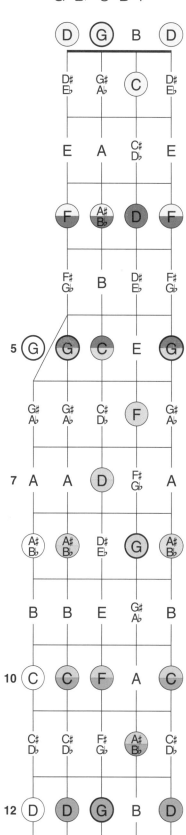

G♯/A♭ MINOR PENTATONIC

G♯–B–C♯–D♯–F♯
A♭–C♭–D♭–E♭–G♭

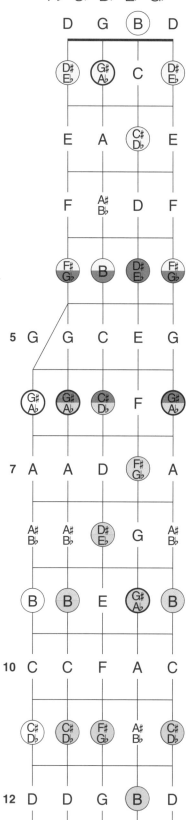

A MINOR PENTATONIC

A–C–D–E–G

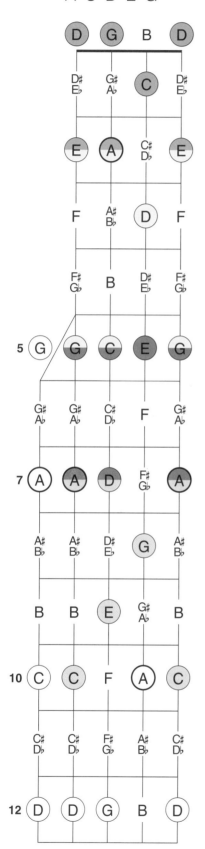

Bb MINOR PENTATONIC

Bb–Db–Eb–F–Ab

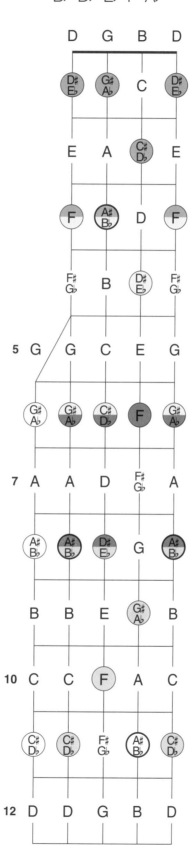

B MINOR PENTATONIC

B–D–E–F#–A

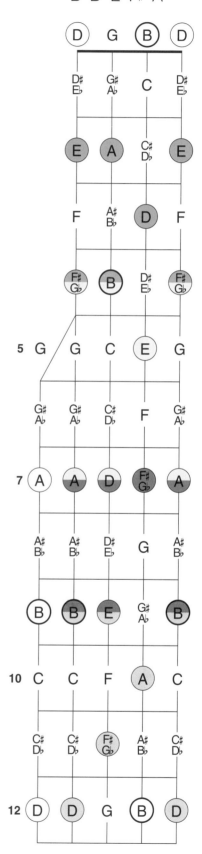

C BLUES

C–E♭–F–G♭–G–B♭

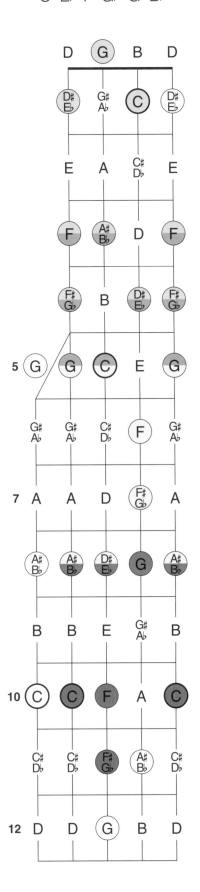

C# BLUES

C#–E–F#–G–G#–B

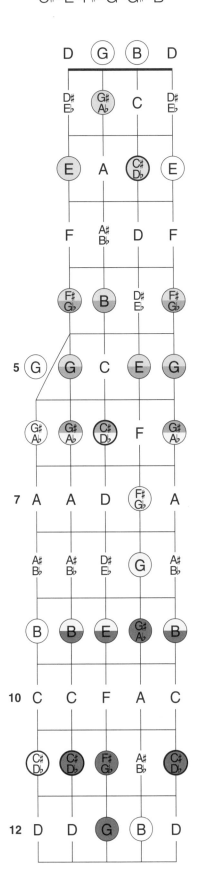

D BLUES

D–F–G–A♭–A–C

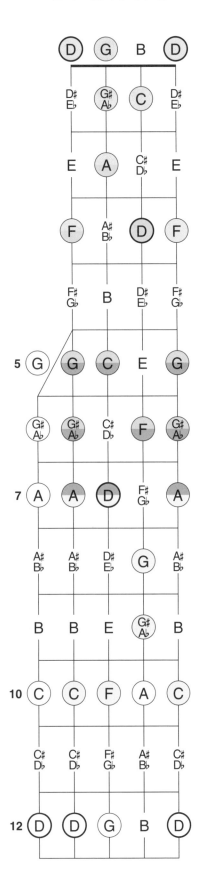

D#/E♭ BLUES

D#–F#–G#–A–A#–C#
E♭–G♭–A♭–A–B♭–D♭

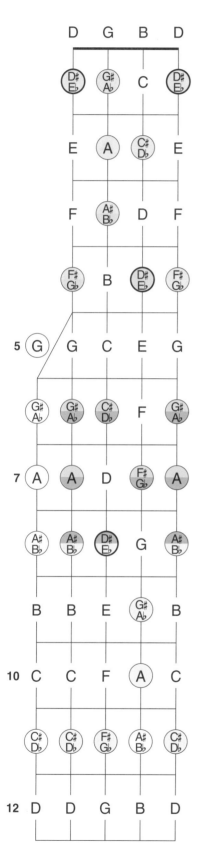

E BLUES

E–G–A–B♭–B–D

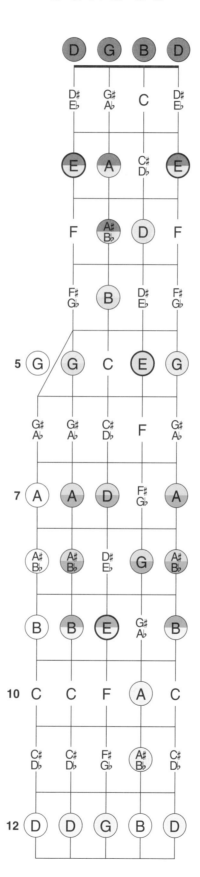

F BLUES

F–A♭–B♭–B–C–E♭

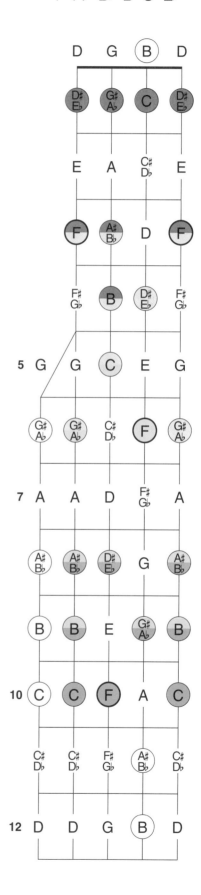

F# BLUES

F#–A–B–C–C#–E

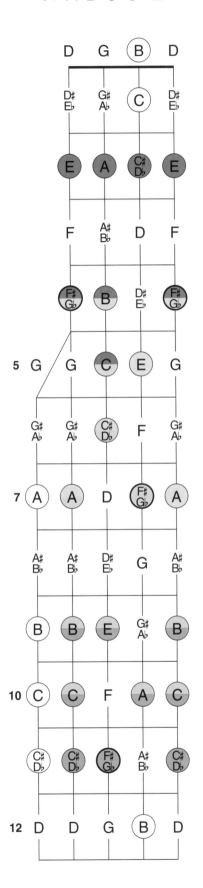

G BLUES

G–B♭–C–D♭–D–F

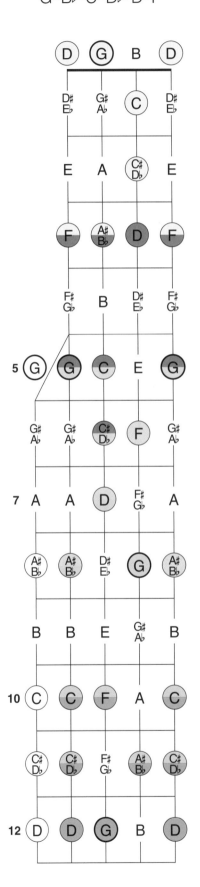

A♭ BLUES

A♭–C♭–D♭–D–E♭–G♭

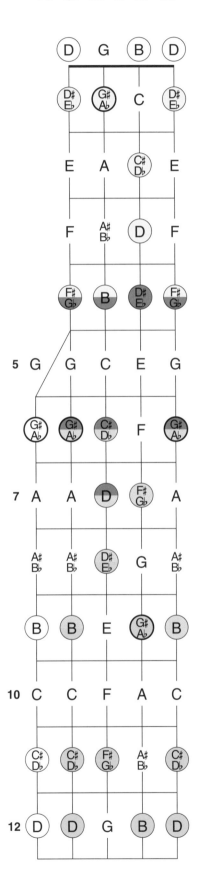

A BLUES

A–C–D–Eb–E–G

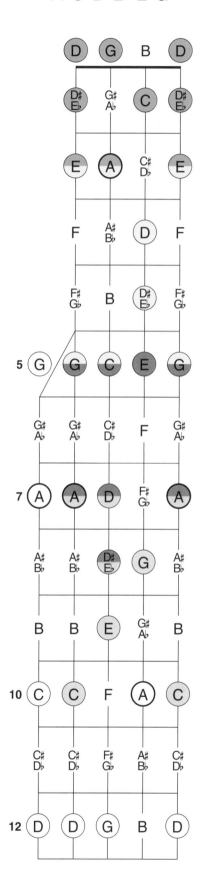

Bb BLUES

Bb–Db–Eb–E–F–Ab

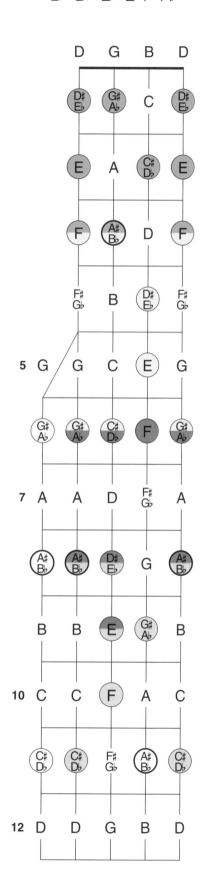

B BLUES

B–D–E–F–F#–A

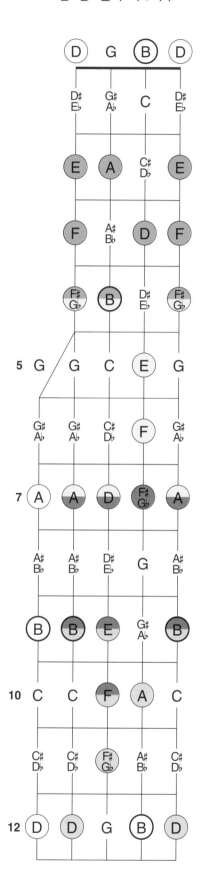

SCALES

THE MELODIC MINOR SCALE AND SELECT MODES

C MELODIC MINOR

C–D–E♭–F–G–A–B

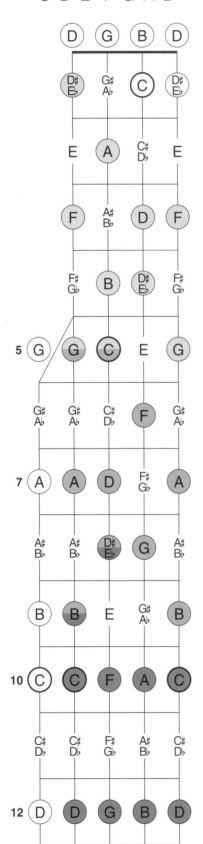

C# MELODIC MINOR

C#–D#–E–F#–G#–A#–B#

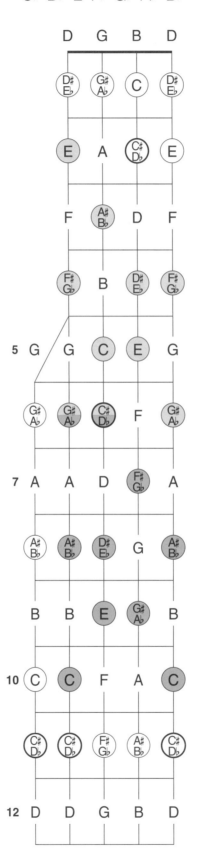

D MELODIC MINOR

D–E–F–G–A–B–C#

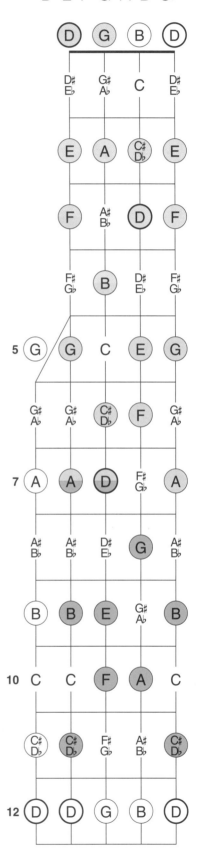

D#/E♭ MELODIC MINOR

D#–E#–F#–G#–A#–B#–C𝄪
E♭–F–G♭–A♭–B♭–C–D

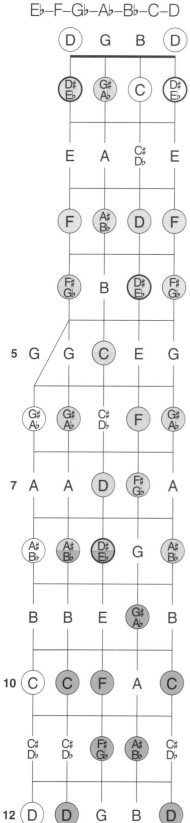

E MELODIC MINOR

E–F#–G–A–B–C#–D#

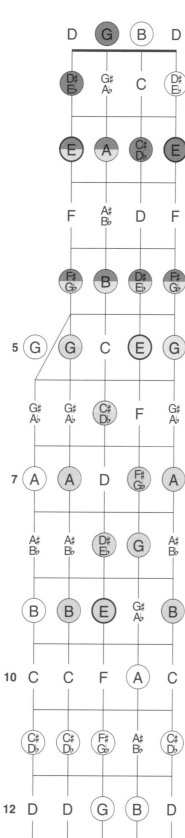

F MELODIC MINOR

F–G–A♭–B♭–C–D–E

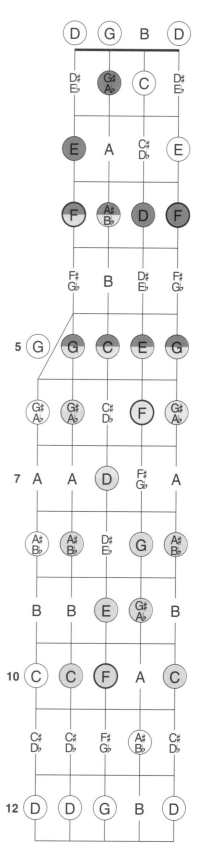

F# MELODIC
MINOR

F#–G#–A–B–C#–D#–E#

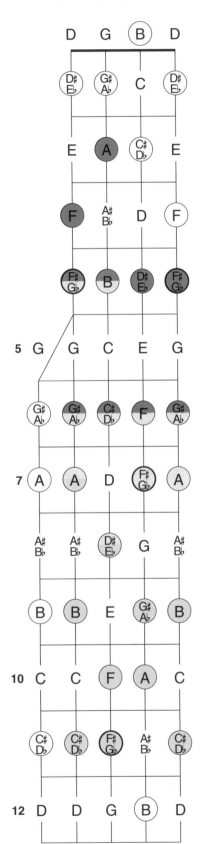

G MELODIC
MINOR

G–A–B♭–C–D–E–F#

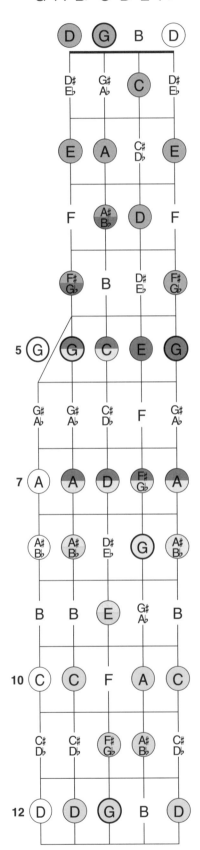

G#/A♭ MELODIC
MINOR

G#–A#–B–C#–D#–E#–F✕
A♭–B♭–C♭–D♭–E♭–F–G

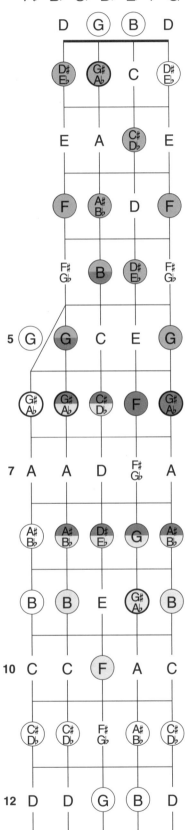

54

A MELODIC MINOR

A–B–C–D–E–F#–G#

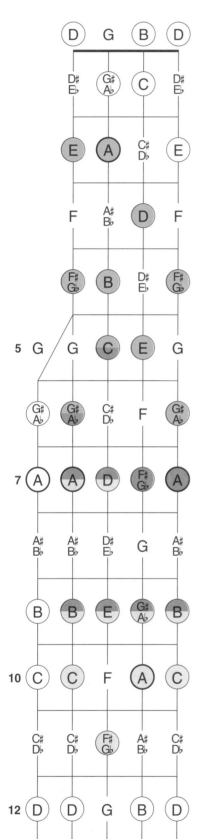

B♭ MELODIC MINOR

B♭–C–D♭–E♭–F–G–A

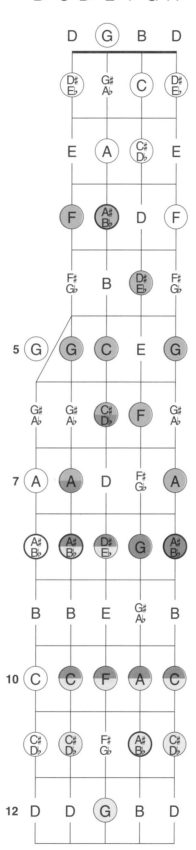

B MELODIC MINOR

B–C#–D–E–F#–G#–A#

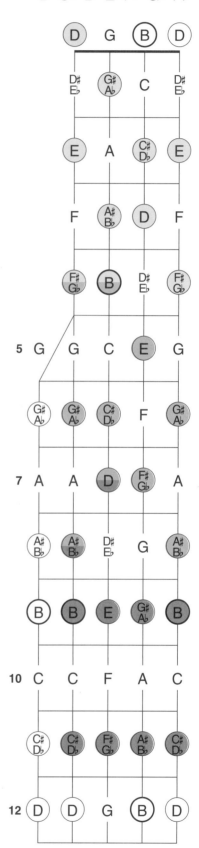

C LYDIAN DOMINANT

C–D–E–F#–G–A–B♭

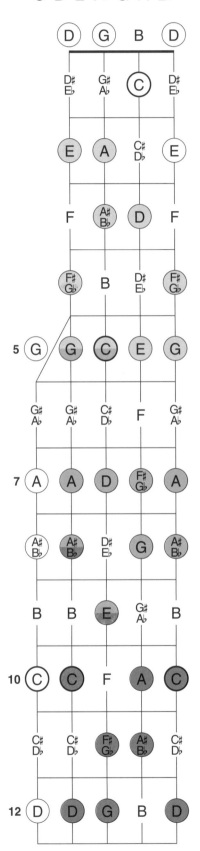

D♭ LYDIAN DOMINANT

D♭–E♭–F–G–A♭–B♭–C♭

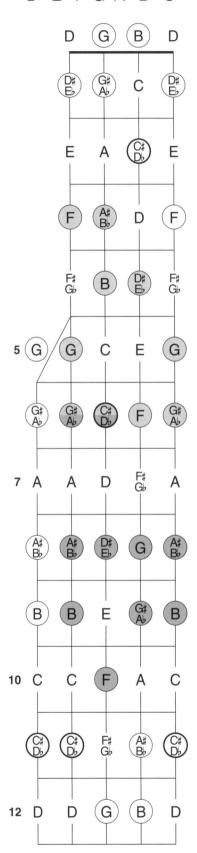

D LYDIAN DOMINANT

D–E–F#–G#–A–B–C

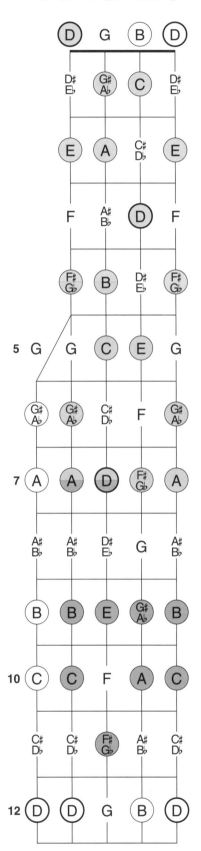

Eb LYDIAN DOMINANT

Eb–F–G–A–Bb–C–Db

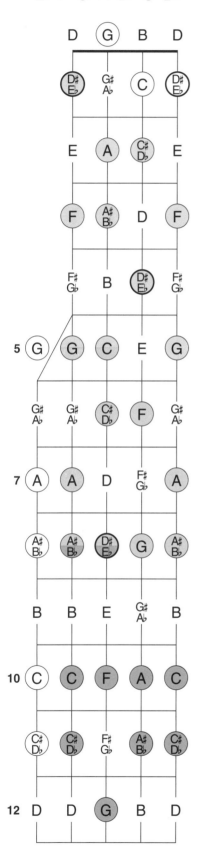

E LYDIAN DOMINANT

E–F#–G#–A#–B–C#–D

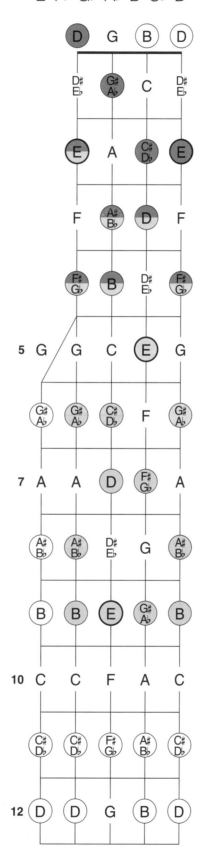

F LYDIAN DOMINANT

F–G–A–B–C–D–Eb

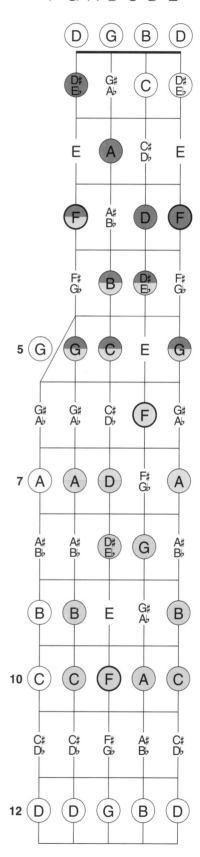

F#/G♭ LYDIAN DOMINANT

F#–G#–A#–B#–C#–D#–E
G♭–A♭–B♭–C–D♭–E♭–F♭

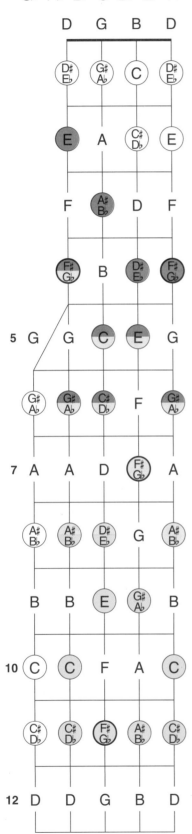

G LYDIAN DOMINANT

G–A–B–C#–D–E–F

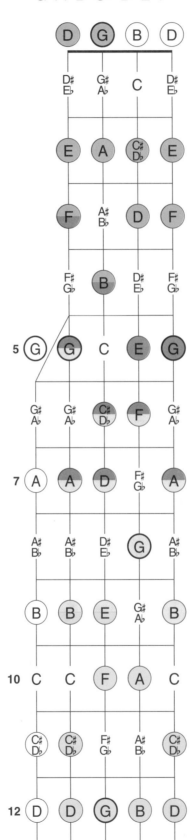

A♭ LYDIAN DOMINANT

A♭–B♭–C–D–E♭–F–G♭

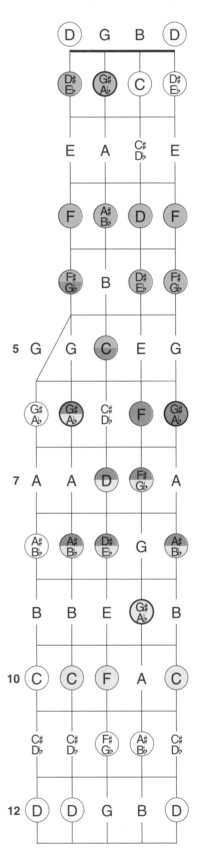

A LYDIAN DOMINANT

A–B–C#–D#–E–F#–G

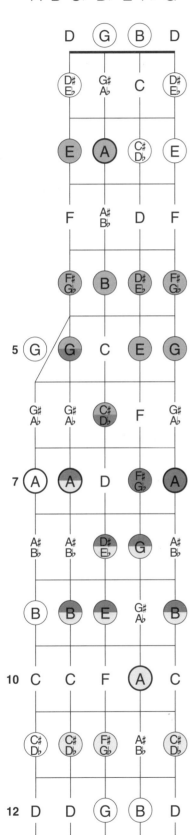

Bb LYDIAN DOMINANT

Bb–C–D–E–F–G–Ab

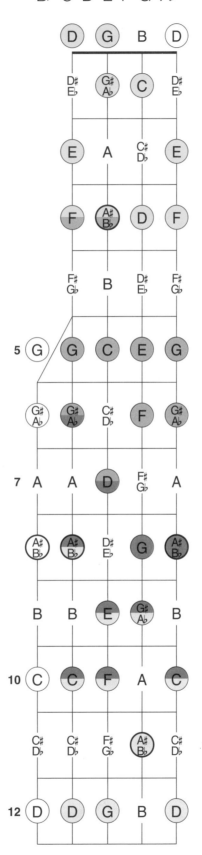

B LYDIAN DOMINANT

B–C#–D#–E#–F#–G#–A

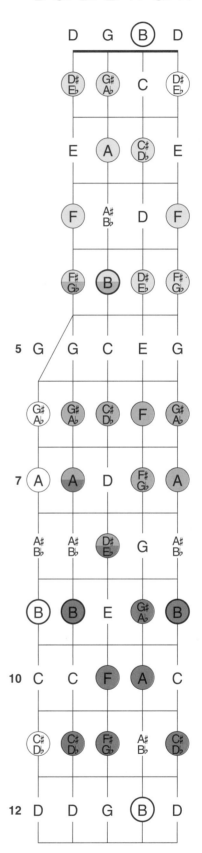

C SUPER LOCRIAN

C–D♭–E♭–F♭–G♭–A♭–B♭

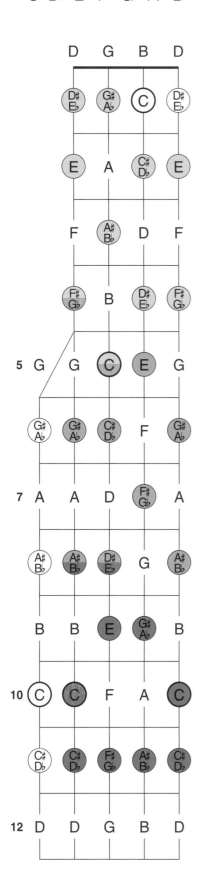

C♯ SUPER LOCRIAN

C♯–D–E–F–G–A–B

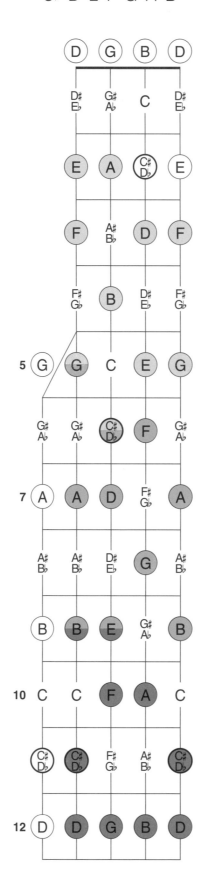

D SUPER LOCRIAN

D–E♭–F–G♭–A♭–B♭–C

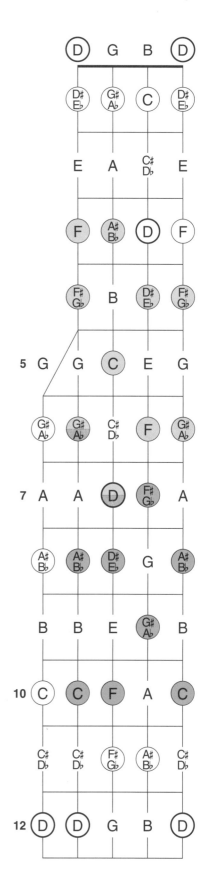

D♯ SUPER LOCRIAN

D♯–E–F♯–G–A–B–C♯

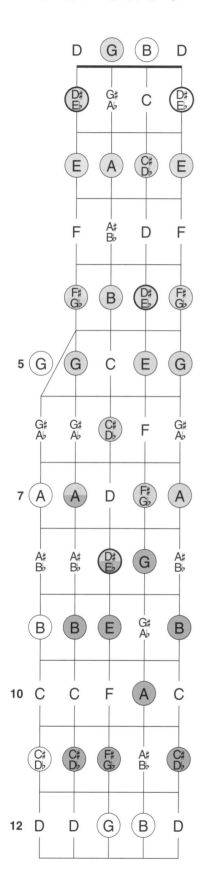

E SUPER LOCRIAN

E–F–G–A♭–B♭–C–D

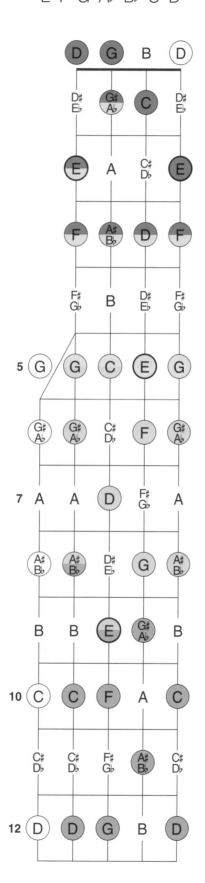

F SUPER LOCRIAN

F–G♭–A♭–B♭♭–C♭–D♭–E♭

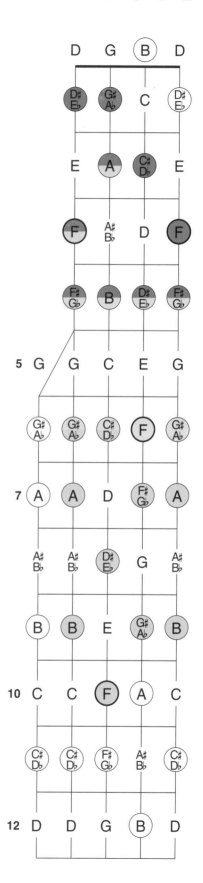

F♯ SUPER LOCRIAN

F♯–G–A–B♭–C–D–E

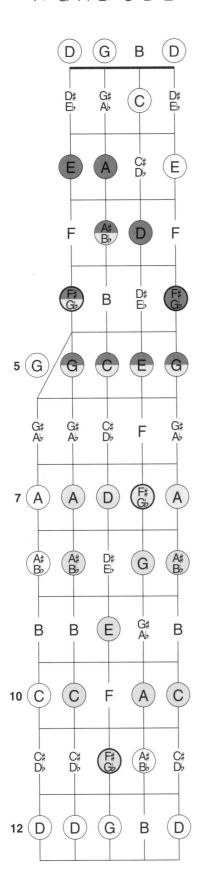

G SUPER LOCRIAN

G–A♭–B♭–C♭–D♭–E♭–F

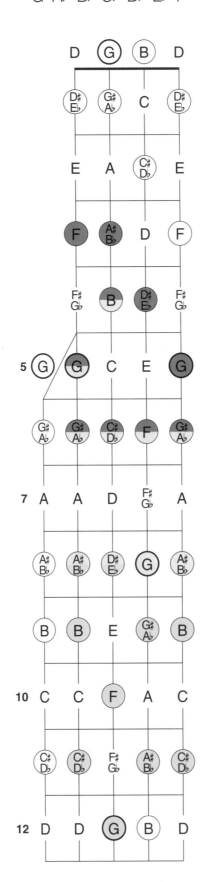

G♯ SUPER LOCRIAN

G♯–A–B–C–D–E–F♯

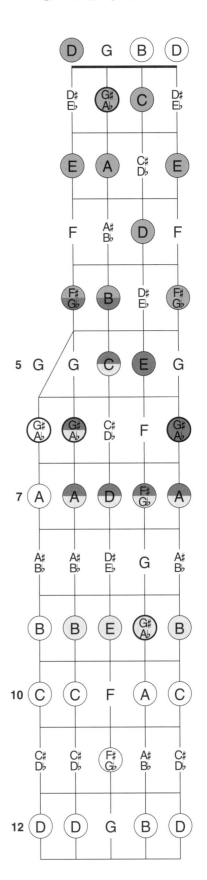

A SUPER LOCRIAN

A–Bb–C–Db–Eb–F–G

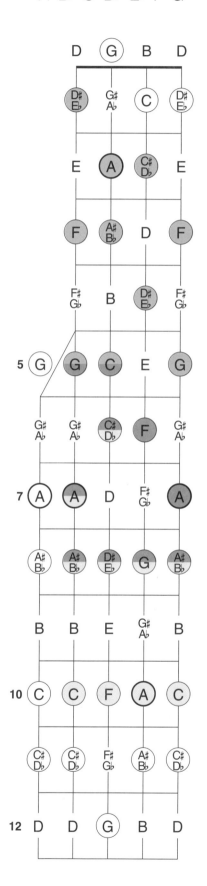

A# SUPER LOCRIAN

A#–B–C#–D–E–F#–G#

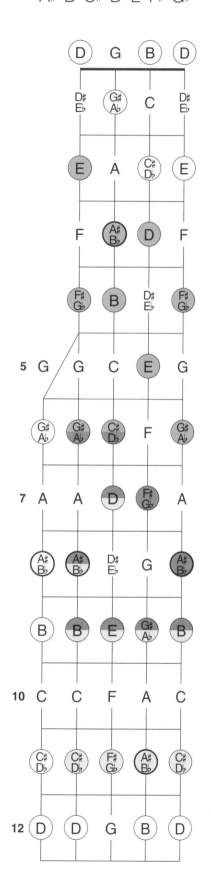

B SUPER LOCRIAN

B–C–D–Eb–F–G–A

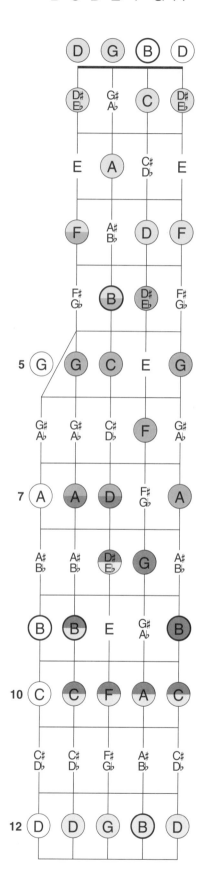

SCALES

THE HARMONIC MINOR SCALE AND SELECT MODE

C HARMONIC MINOR

C–D–E♭–F–G–A♭–B

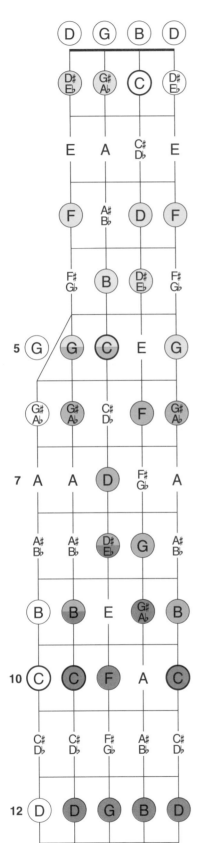

C♯ HARMONIC MINOR

C♯–D♯–E–F♯–G♯–A–B♯

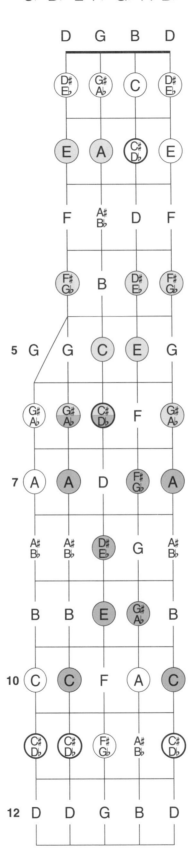

D HARMONIC MINOR

D–E–F–G–A–B♭–C♯

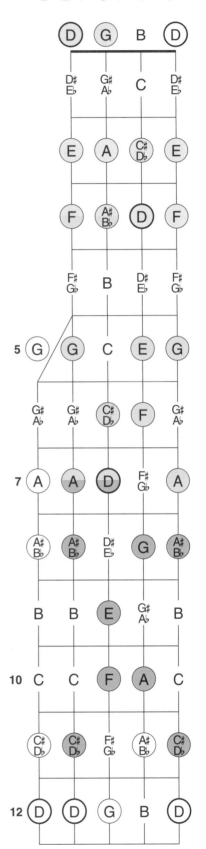

E♭ HARMONIC MINOR

E♭–F–G♭–A♭–B♭–C♭–D

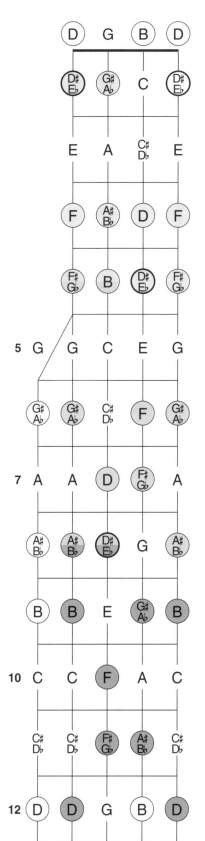

E HARMONIC MINOR

E–F♯–G–A–B–C–D♯

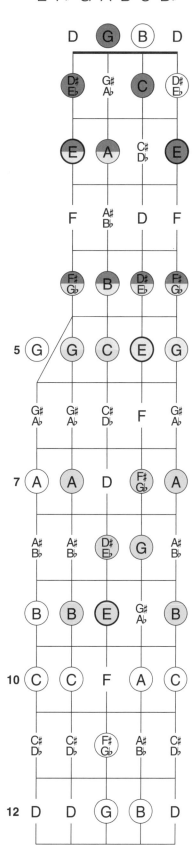

F HARMONIC MINOR

F–G–A♭–B♭–C–D♭–E

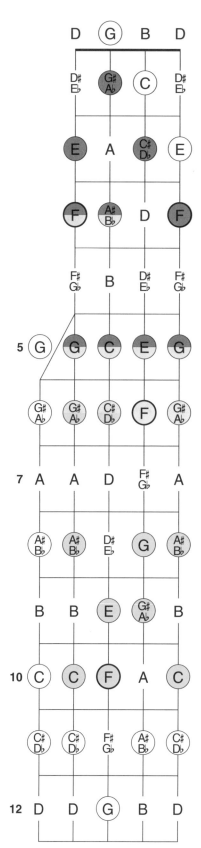

F# HARMONIC MINOR

F#–G#–A–B–C#–D–E#

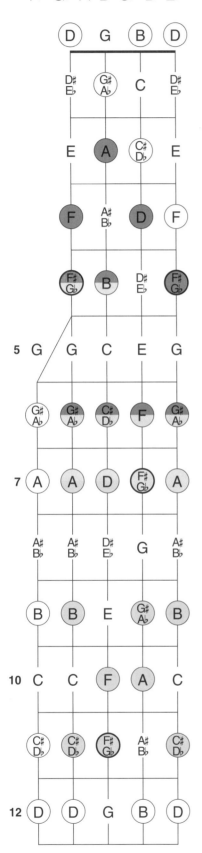

G HARMONIC MINOR

G–A–Bb–C–D–Eb–F#

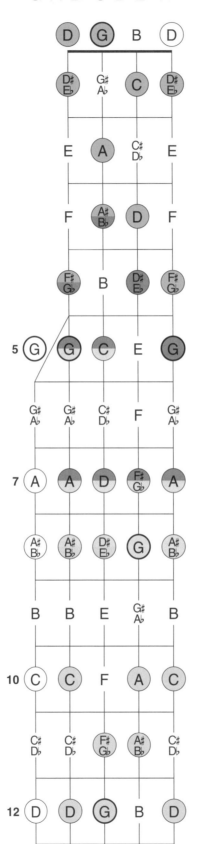

Ab HARMONIC MINOR

Ab–Bb–Cb–Db–Eb–Fb–G

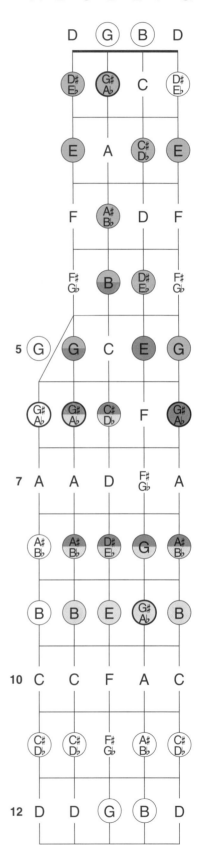

A HARMONIC MINOR

A–B–C–D–E–F–G♯

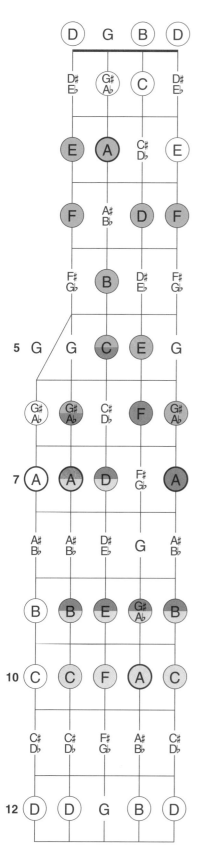

B♭ HARMONIC MINOR

B♭–C–D♭–E♭–F–G♭–A

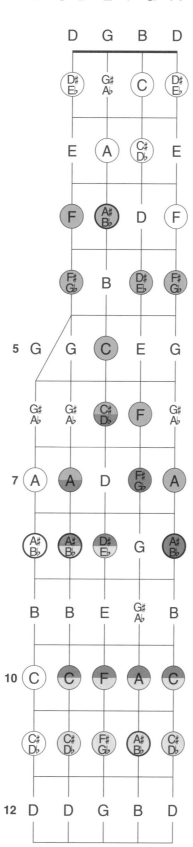

B HARMONIC MINOR

B–C♯–D–E–F♯–G–A♯

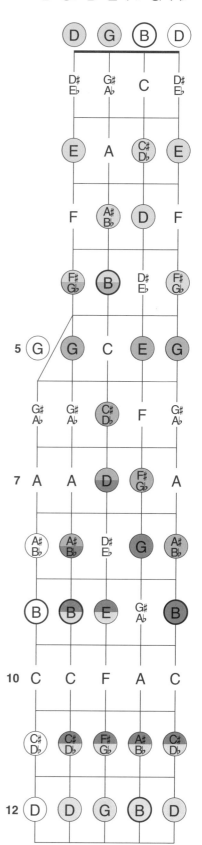

C PHRYGIAN DOMINANT

C–Db–E–F–G–Ab–Bb

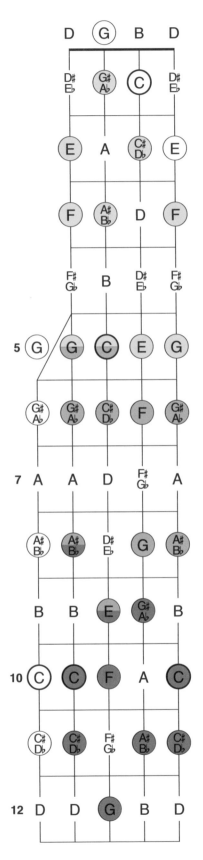

C# PHRYGIAN DOMINANT

C#–D–E#–F#–G#–A–B

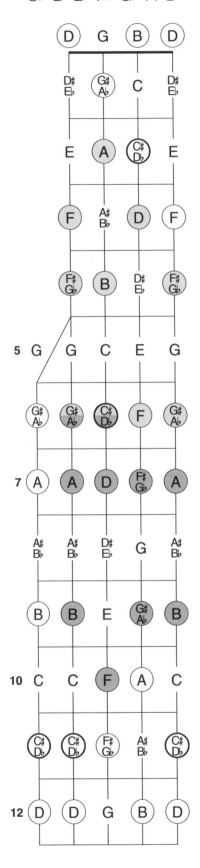

D PHRYGIAN DOMINANT

D–Eb–F#–G–A–Bb–C

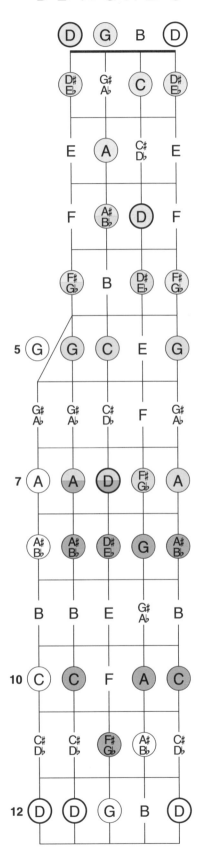

E♭ PHRYGIAN DOMINANT

E♭–F♭–G–A♭–B♭–C♭–D♭

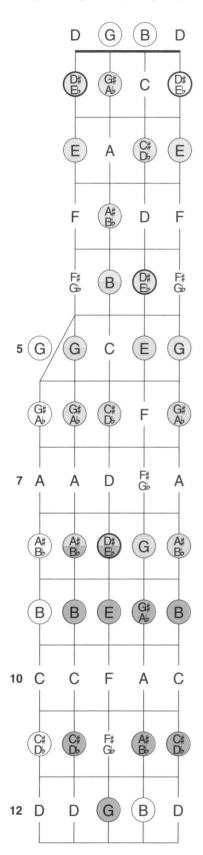

E PHRYGIAN DOMINANT

E–F–G♯–A–B–C–D

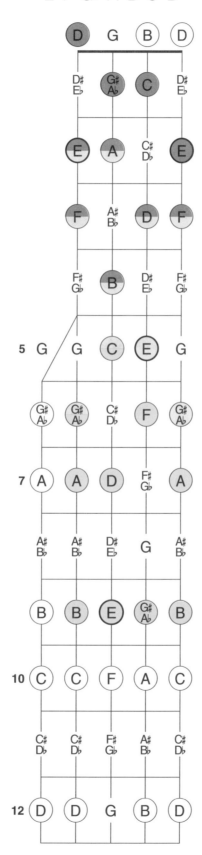

F PHRYGIAN DOMINANT

F–G♭–A–B♭–C–D♭–E♭

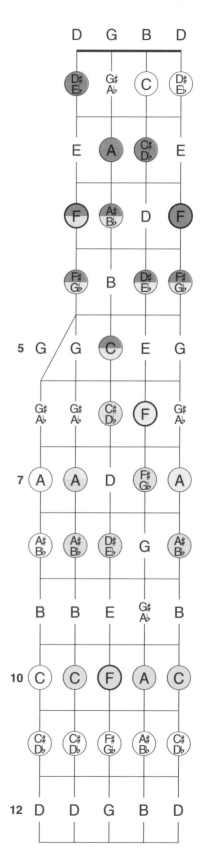

F♯ PHRYGIAN DOMINANT

F♯–G–A♯–B–C♯–D–E

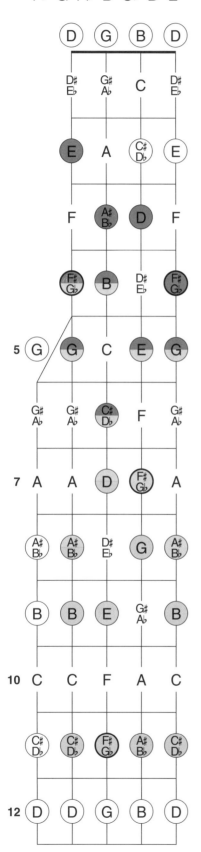

G PHRYGIAN DOMINANT

G–A♭–B–C–D–E♭–F

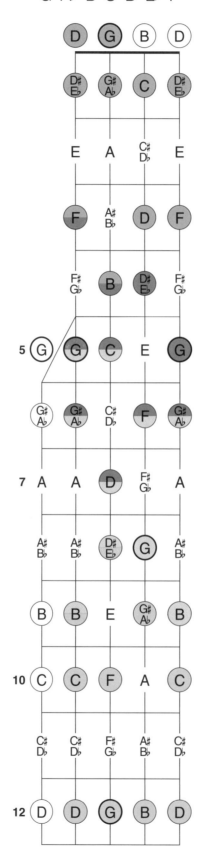

G♯ PHRYGIAN DOMINANT

G♯–A–B♯–C♯–D♯–E–F♯

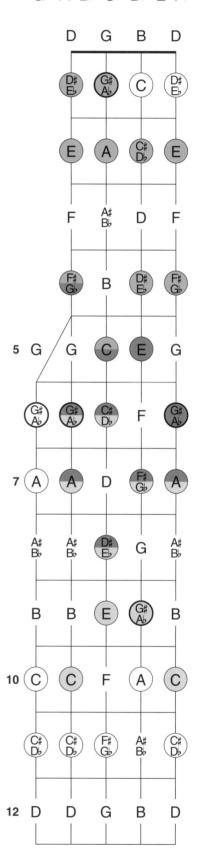

A PHRYGIAN DOMINANT

A–B♭–C♯–D–E–F–G

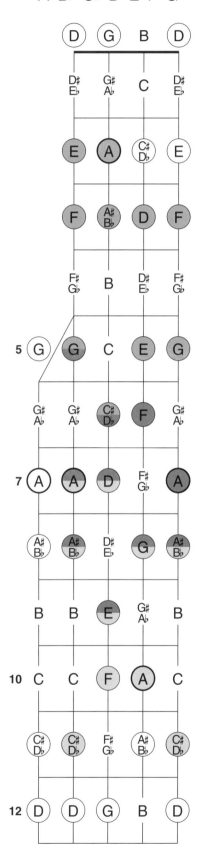

B♭ PHRYGIAN DOMINANT

B♭–C♭–D–E♭–F–G♭–A♭

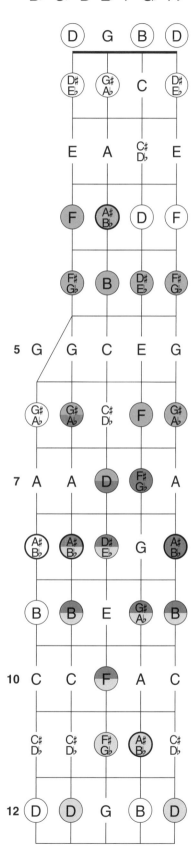

B PHRYGIAN DOMINANT

B–C–D♯–E–F♯–G–A

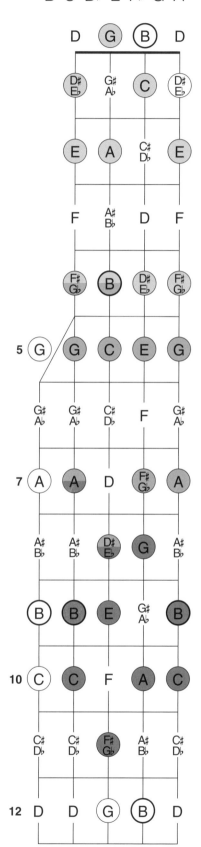

CHORDS
POWER CHORDS

C5

C–G

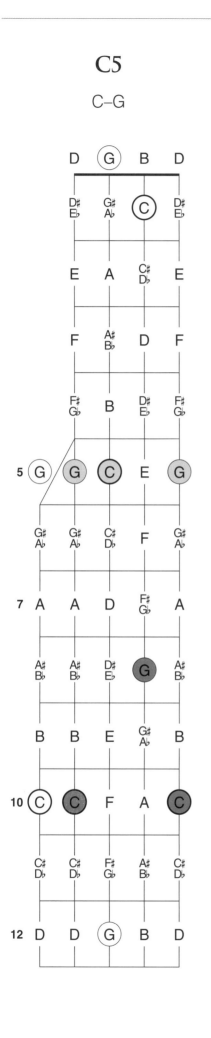

C#/Db5

C#–G#/Db–Ab

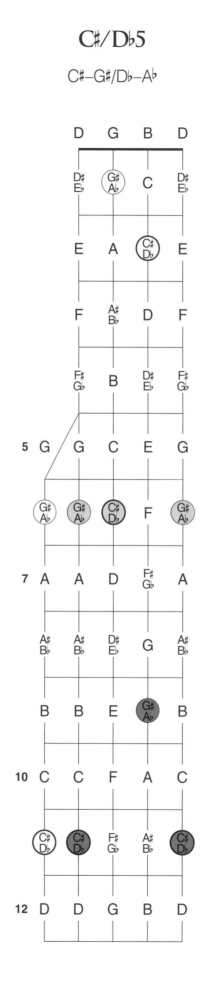

D5

D–A

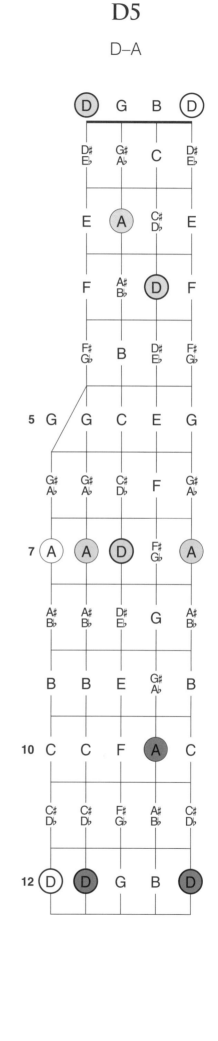

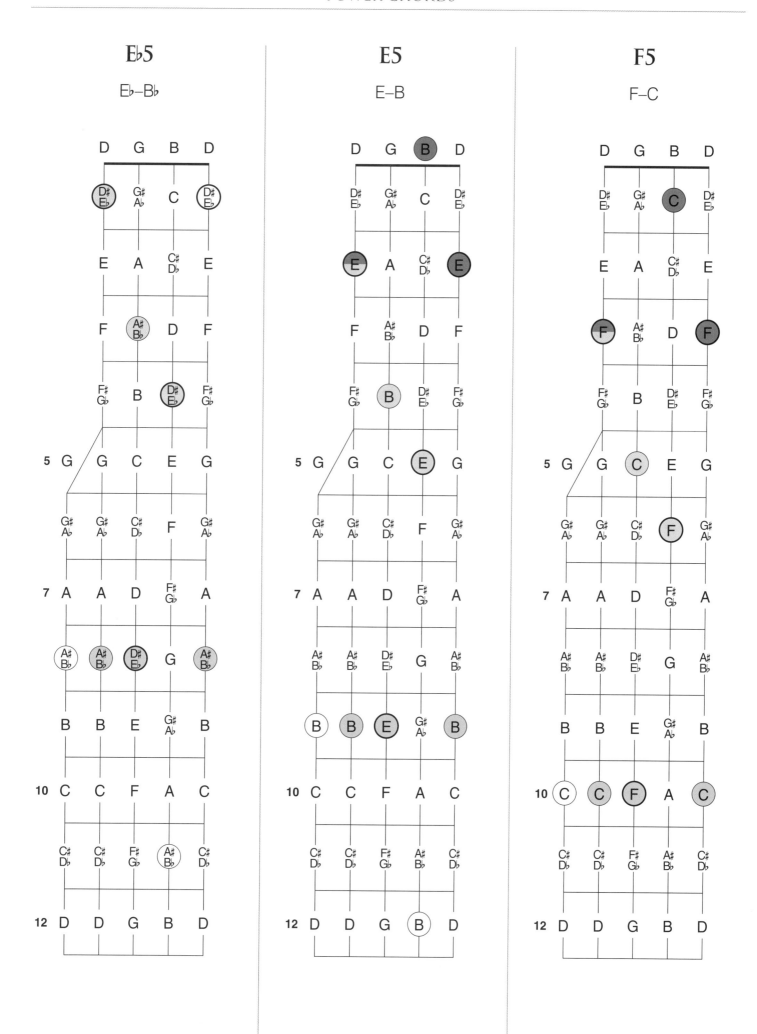

F#/Gb5

F#–C#/Gb–Db

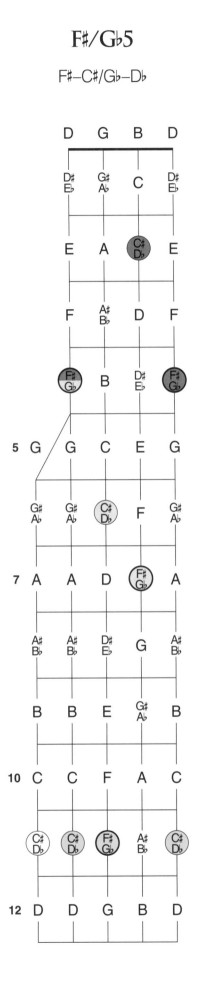

G5

G–D

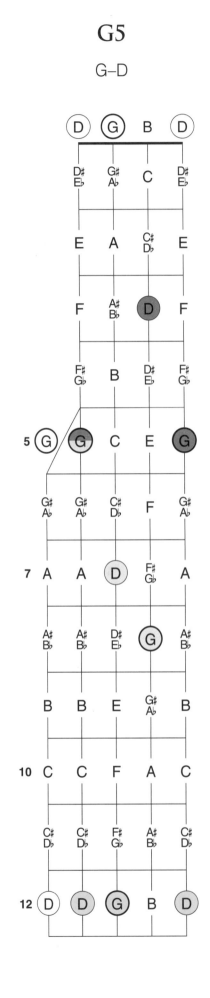

G#/Ab5

G#–D#/Ab–Eb

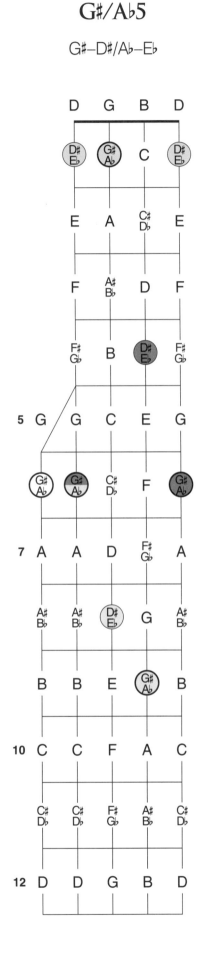

A5

A–E

Bb5

Bb–F

B5

B–F#

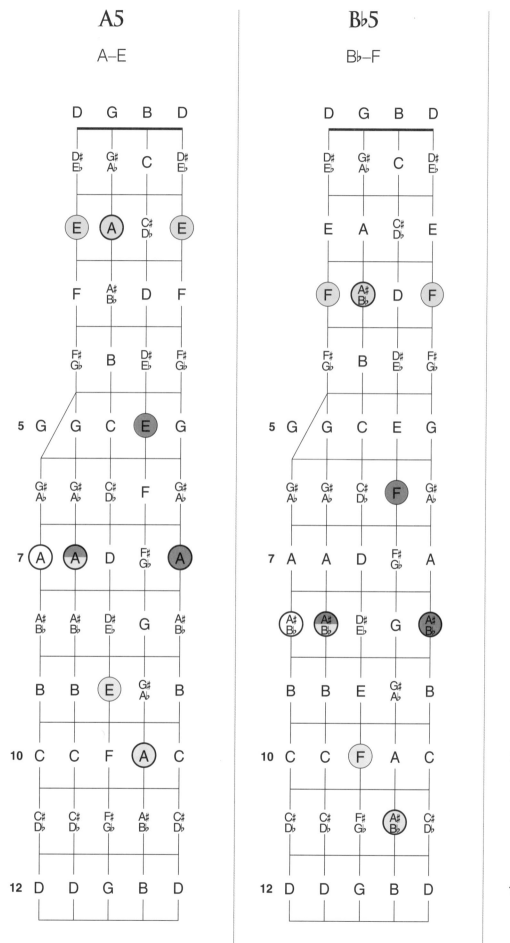

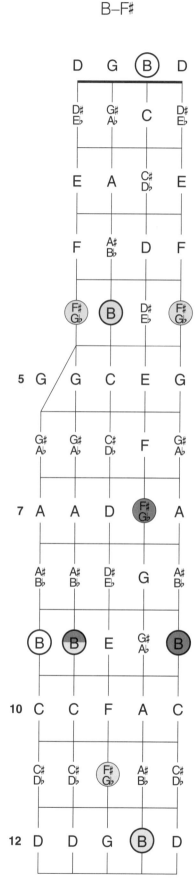

CHORDS
TRIADS

C

C–E–G

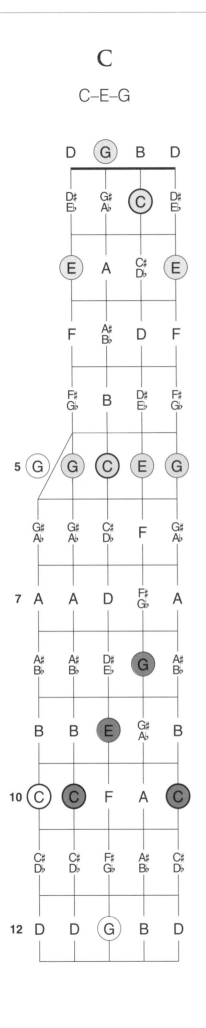

C#/Db

C#–E#–G#/Db–F–Ab

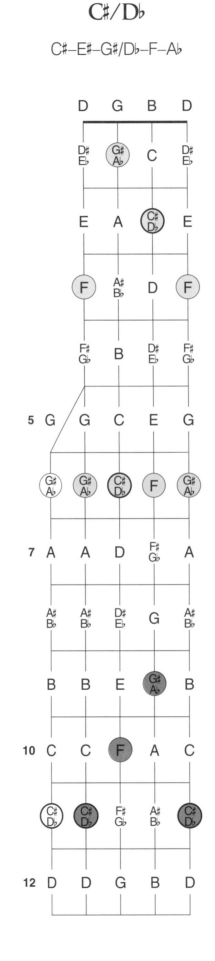

D

D–F#–A

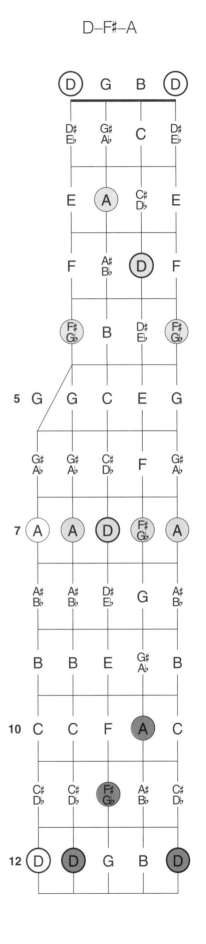

E♭

E♭–G–B♭

E

E–G♯–B

F

F–A–C

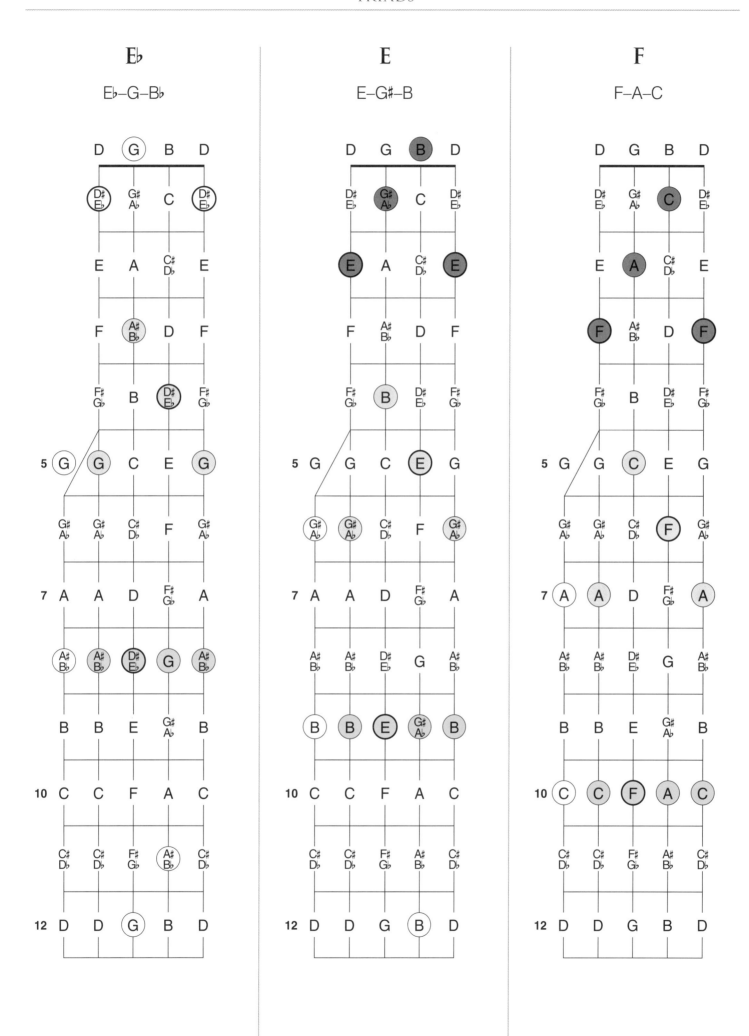

F♯/G♭

F♯–A♯–C♯/G♭–B♭–D♭

G

G–B–D

A♭

A♭–C–E♭

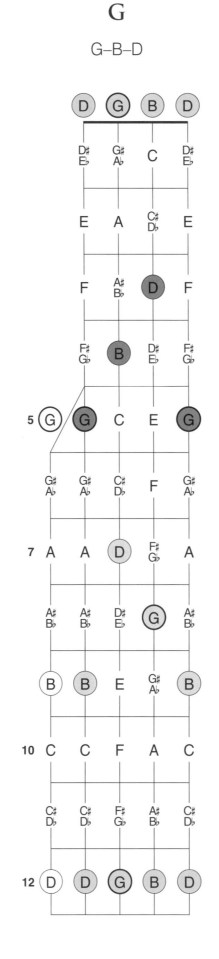

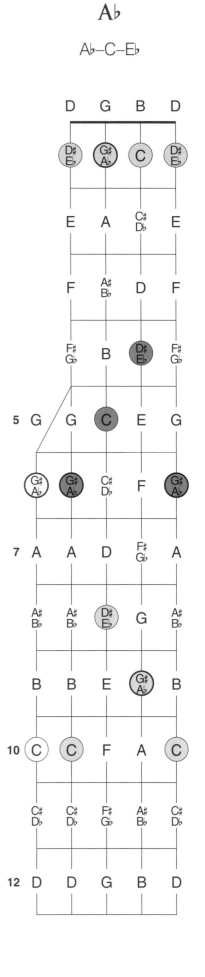

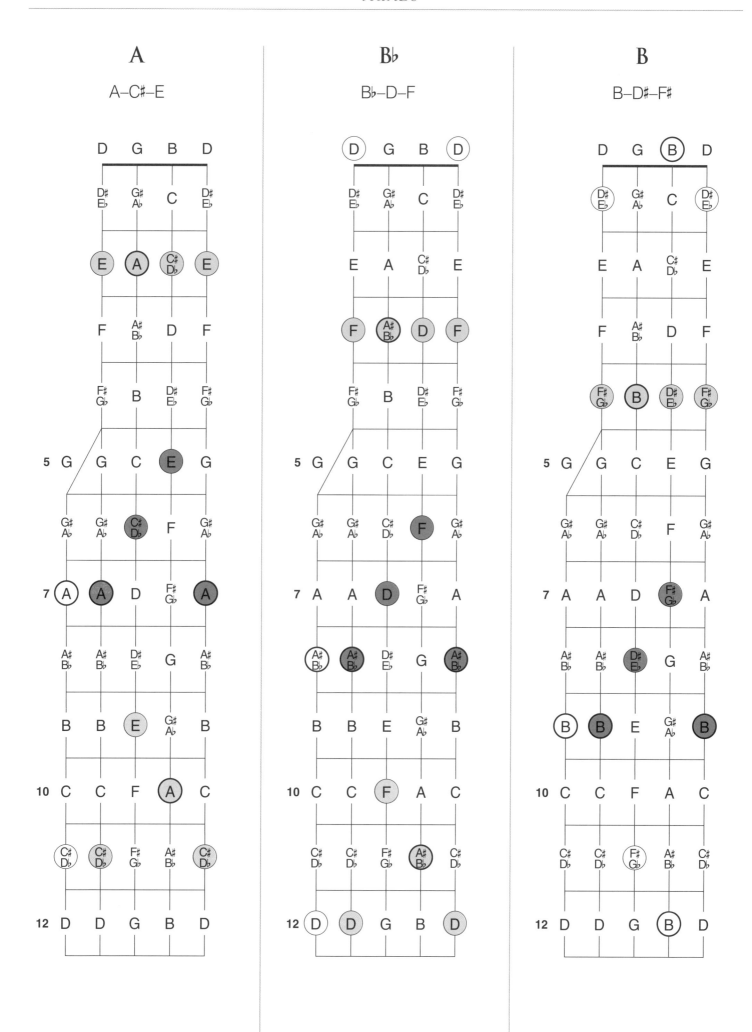

Csus4

C–F–G

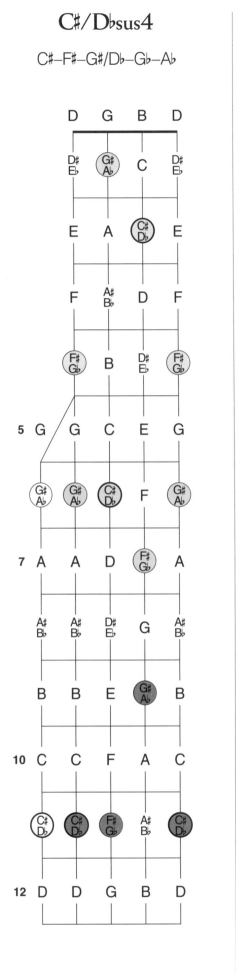

C♯/D♭sus4

C♯–F♯–G♯/D♭–G♭–A♭

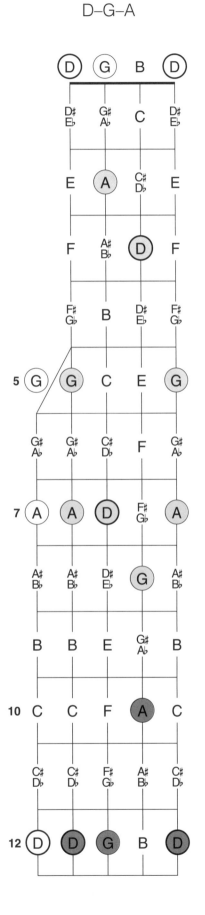

Dsus4

D–G–A

E♭sus4

E♭–A♭–B♭

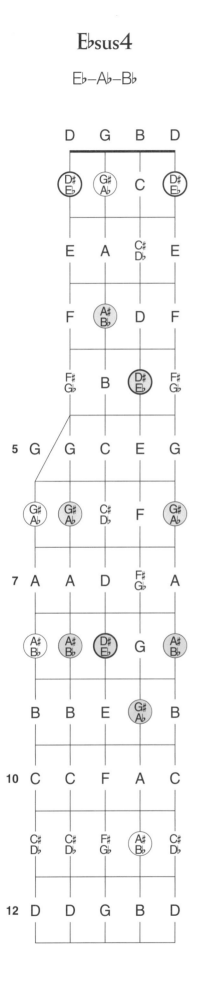

Esus4

E–A–B

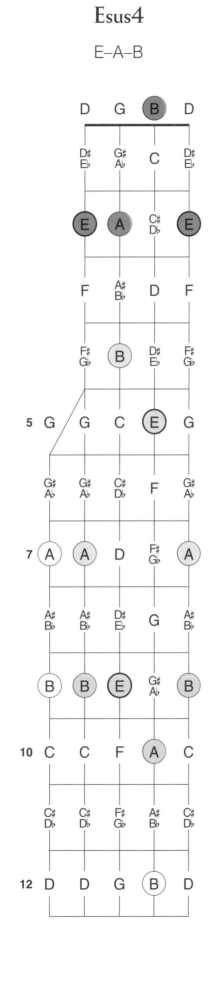

Fsus4

F–B♭–C

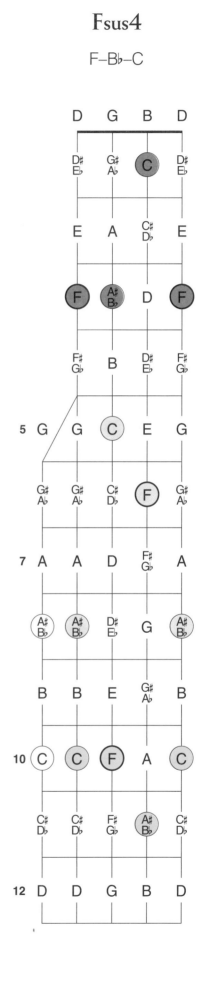

F#/G♭sus4

F#–B–C#/G♭–C♭–D♭

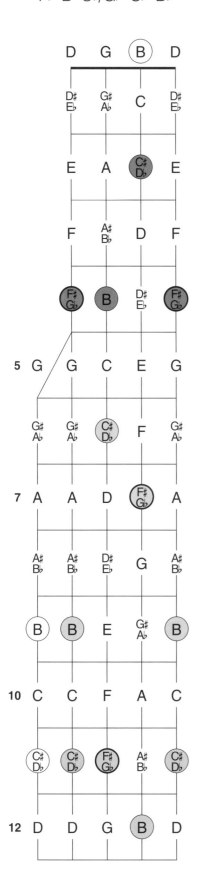

Gsus4

G–C–D

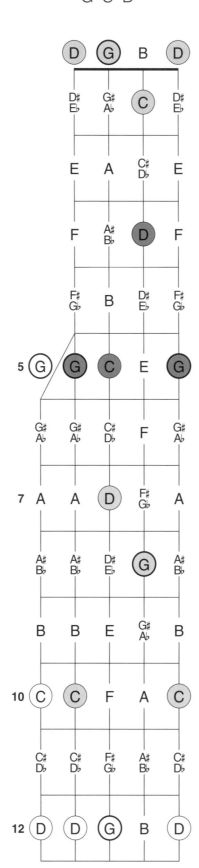

A♭sus4

A♭–D♭–E♭

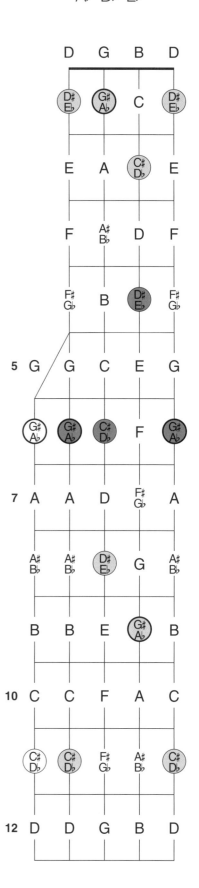

Asus4

A–D–E

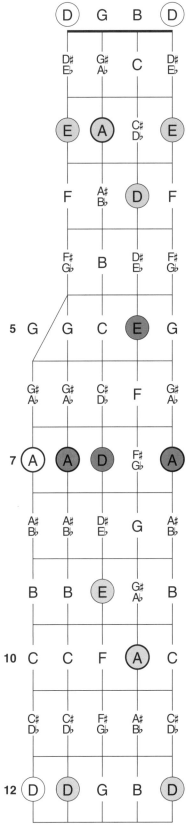

B♭sus4

B♭–E♭–F

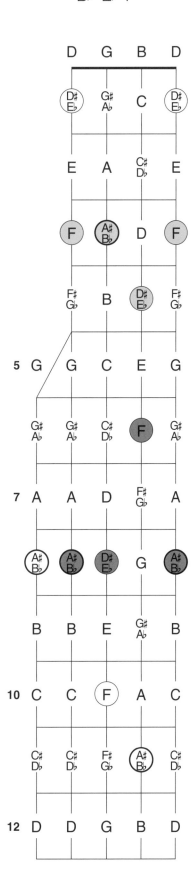

Bsus4

B–E–F♯

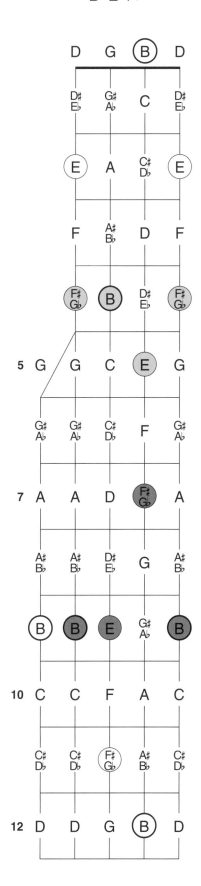

Cm

C–E♭–G

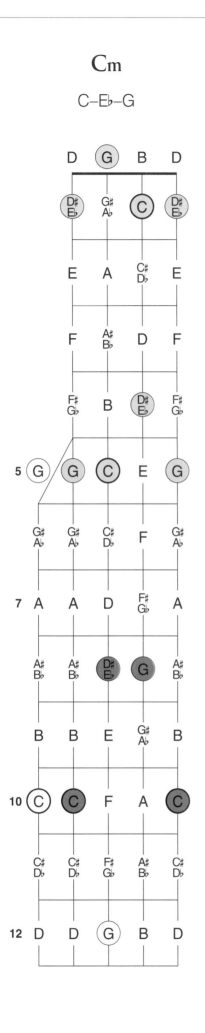

C♯m

C♯–E–G♯

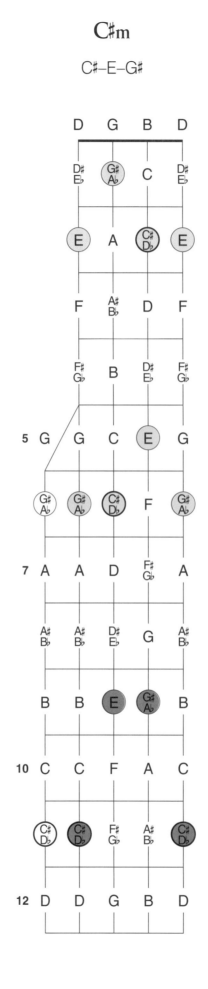

Dm

D–F–A

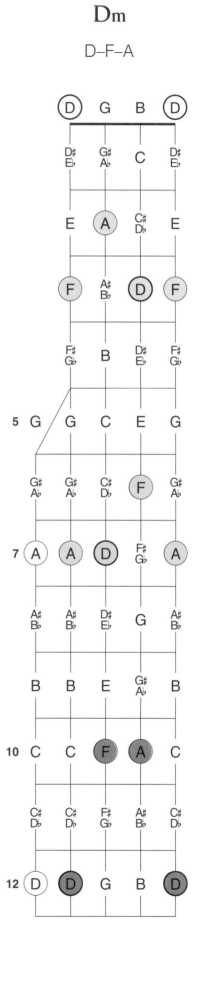

D#/E♭m

D#–F#–A#/E♭–G♭–B♭

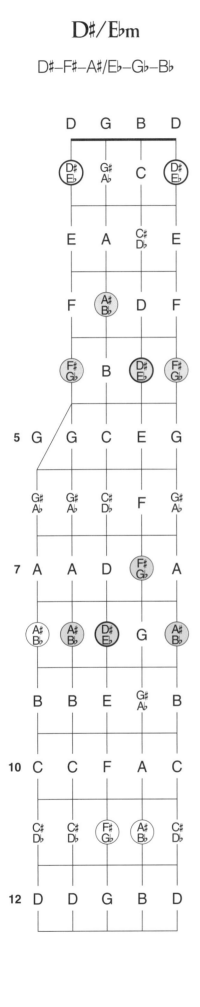

Em

E–G–B

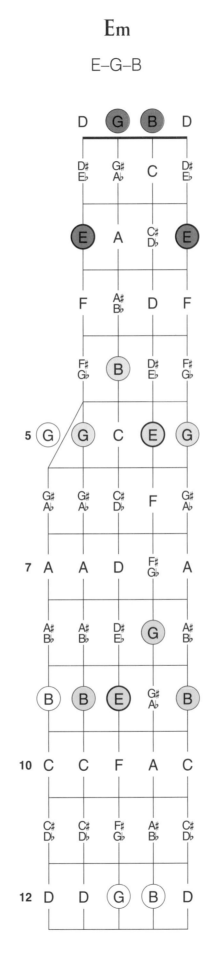

Fm

F–A♭–C

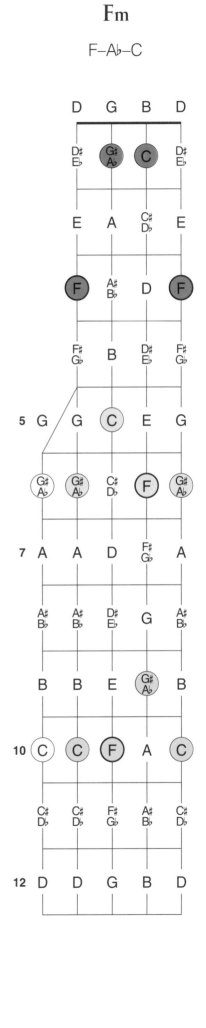

F#m

F#–A–C#

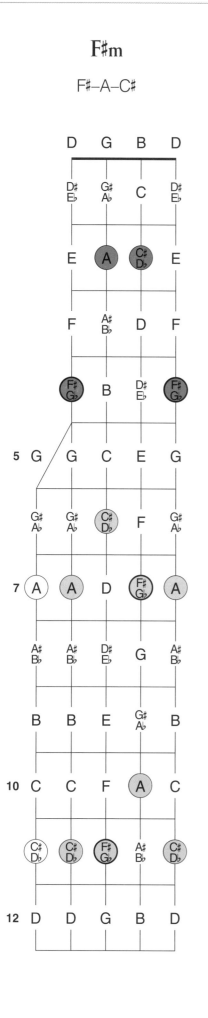

Gm

G–Bb–D

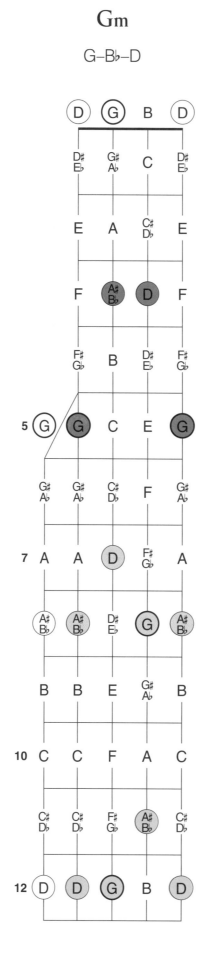

G#/Abm

G#–B–D#/Ab–Cb–Eb

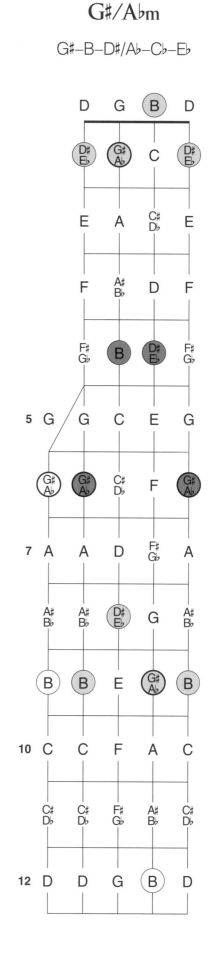

Am

A–C–E

B♭m

B♭–D♭–F

Bm

B–D–F♯

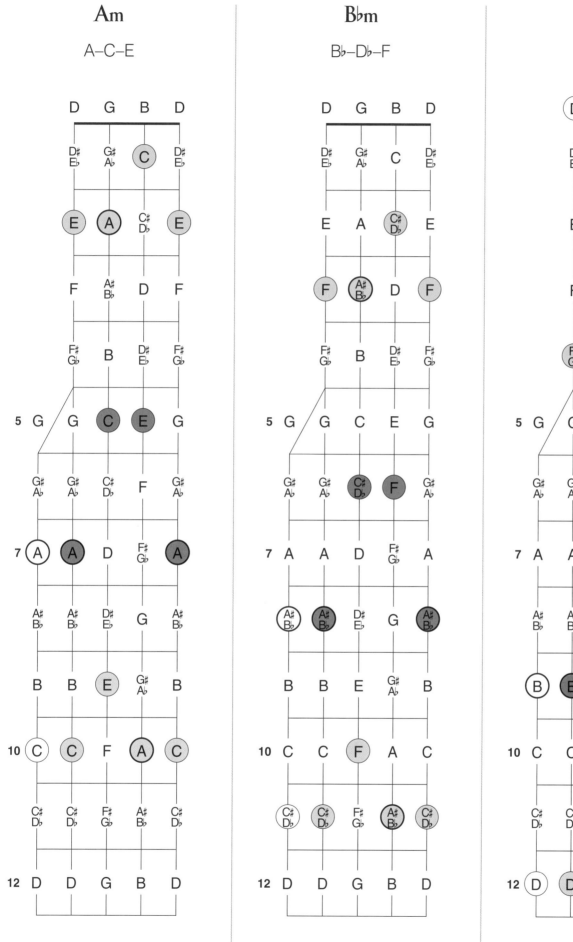
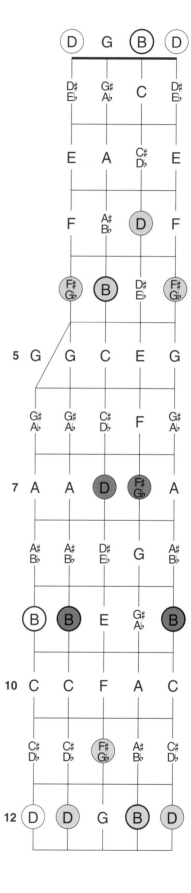

C+

C–E–G#

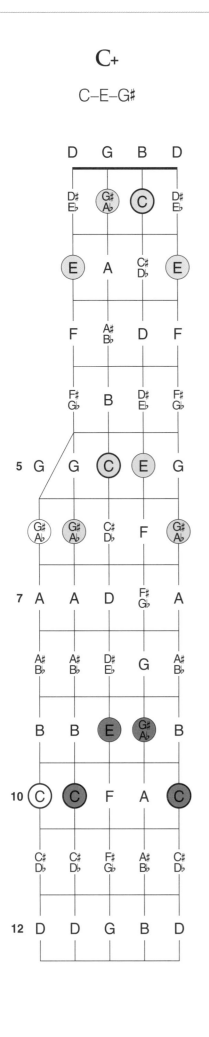

C#/D♭+

C#–E#–G×/D♭–F–A

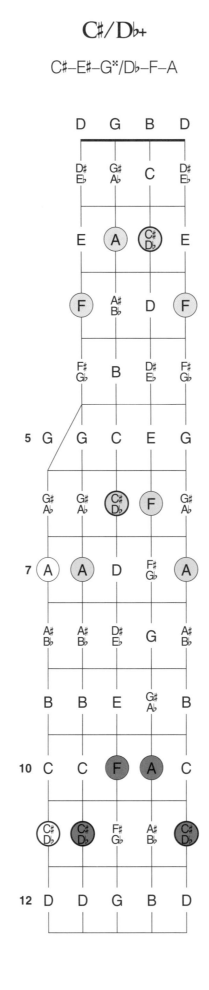

D+

D–F#–A#

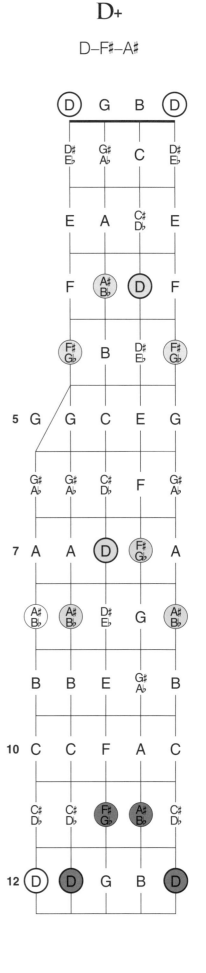

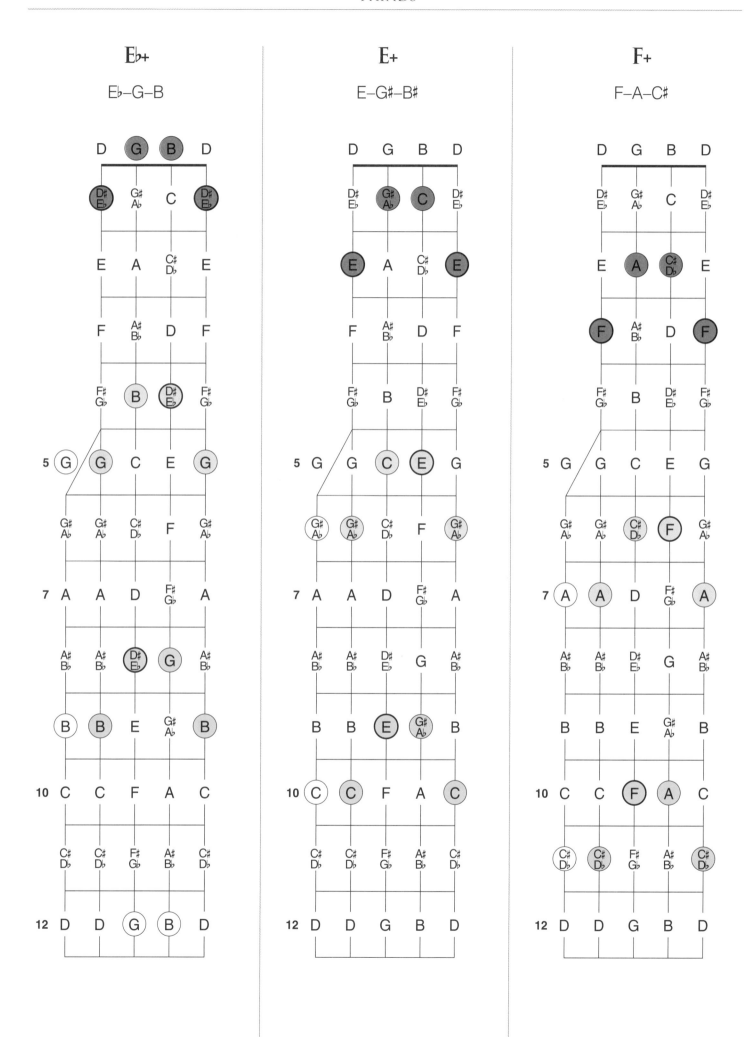

Gb+

Gb–Bb–D

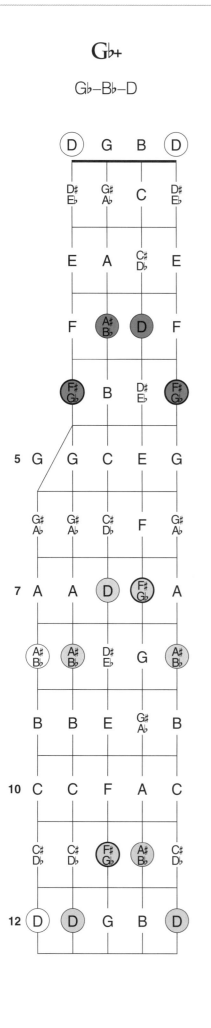

G+

G–B–D#

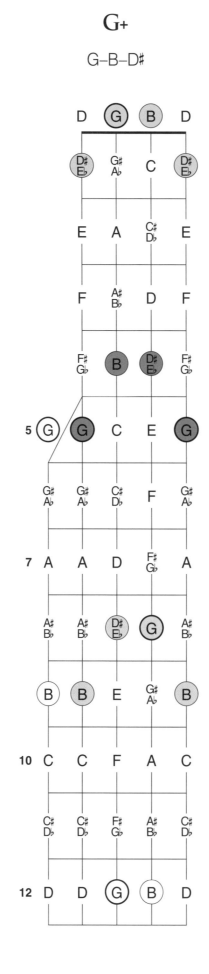

Ab+

Ab–C–E

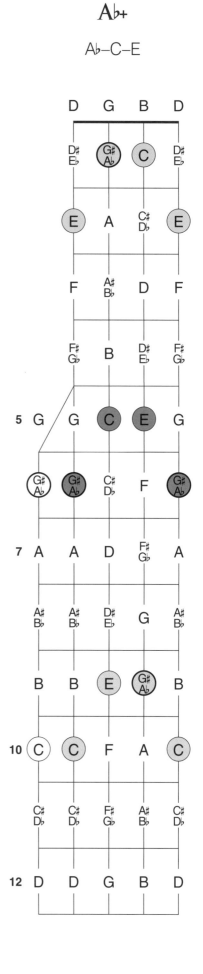

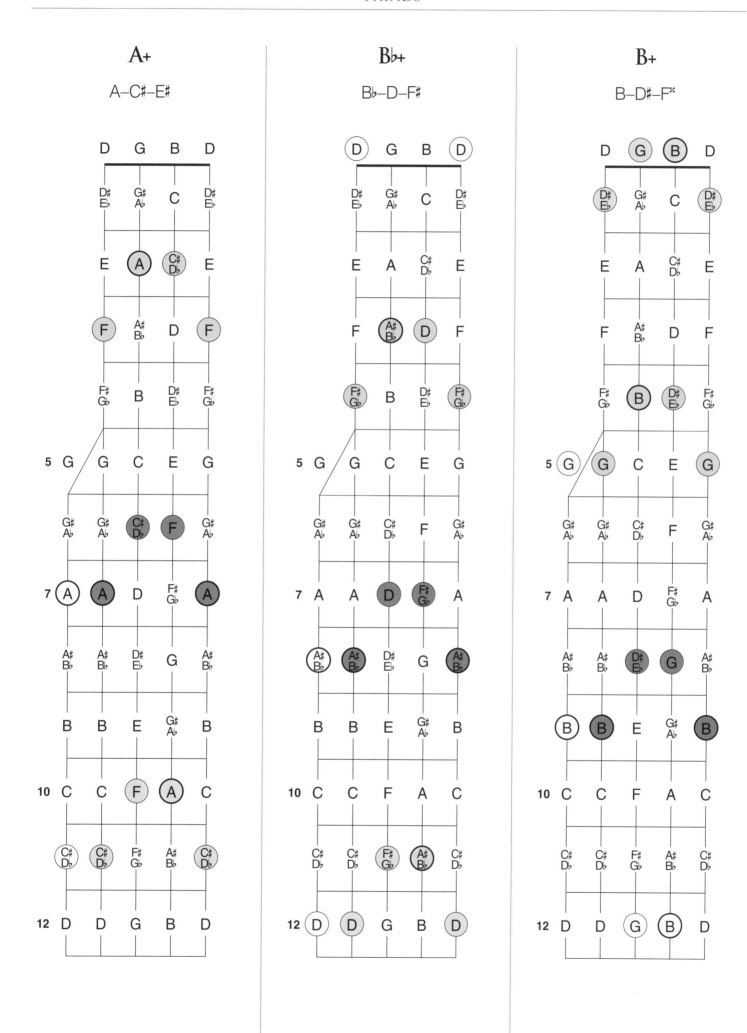

A+

A–C#–E#

Bb+

Bb–D–F#

B+

B–D#–F✕

C°

C–E♭–G♭

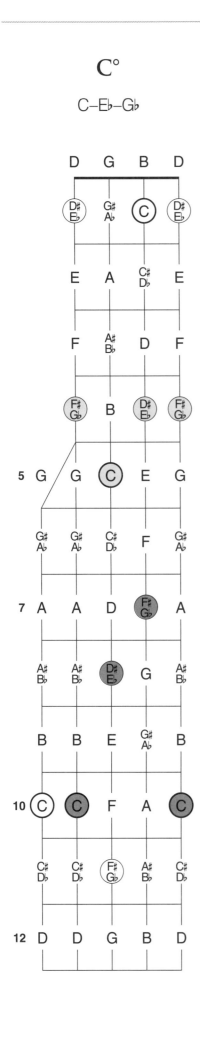

C#°

C#–E–G

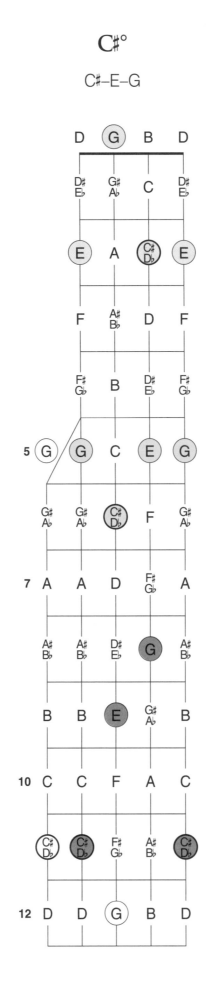

D°

D–F–A♭

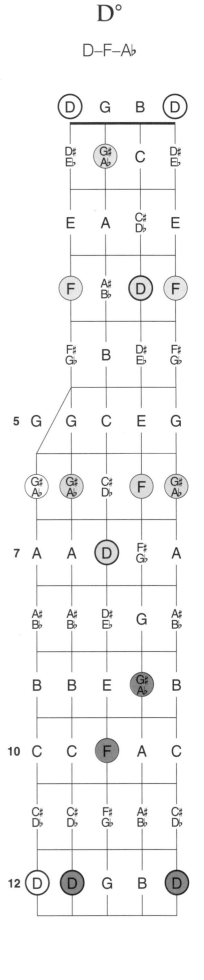

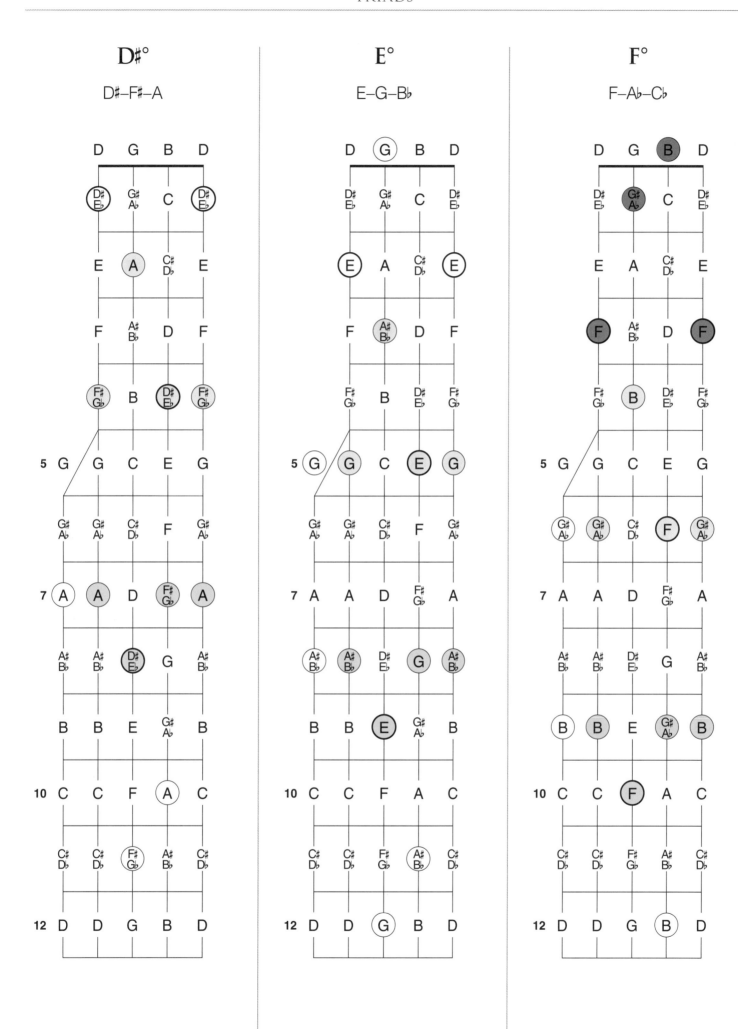

F#°

F#–A–C

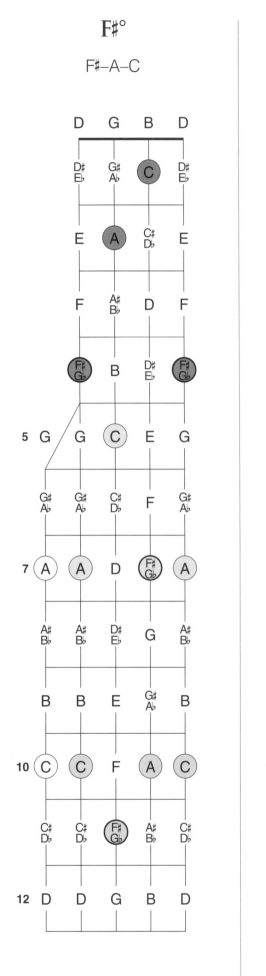

G°

G–B♭–D♭

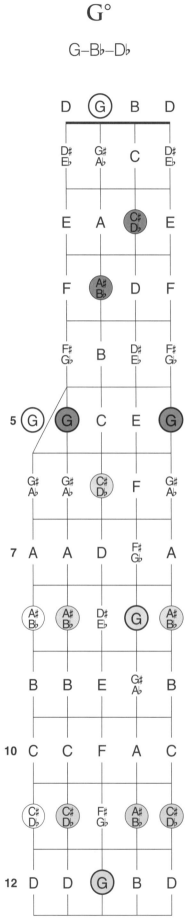

G#°

G#–B–D

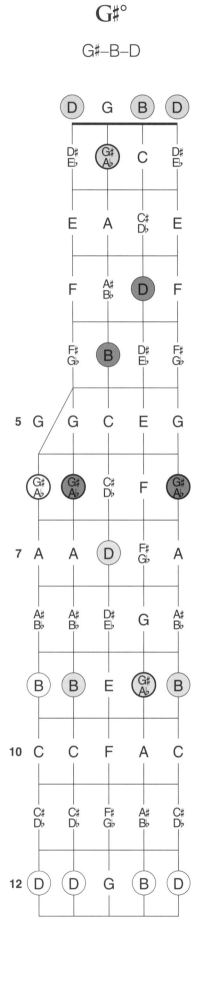

A°

A–C–E♭

B♭°

B♭–D♭–F♭

B°

B–D–F

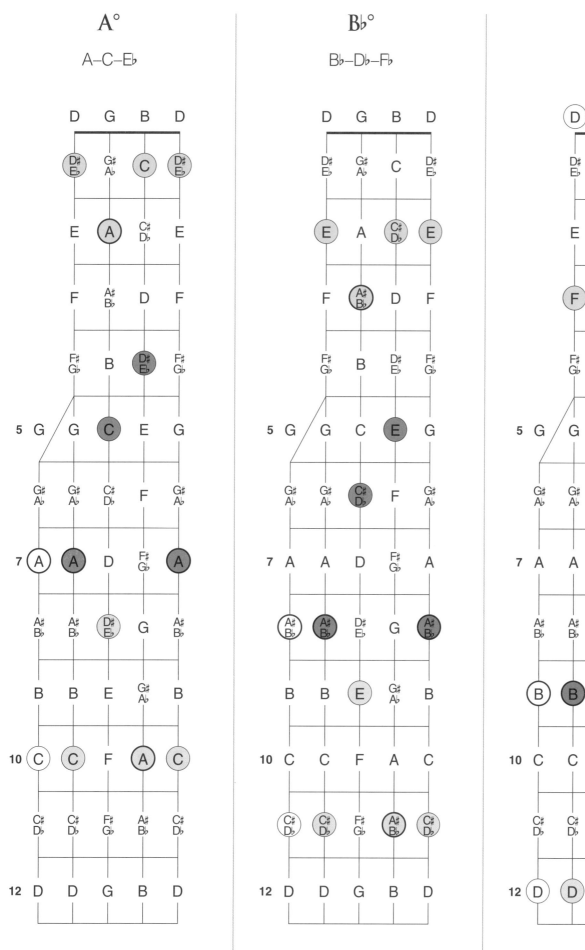
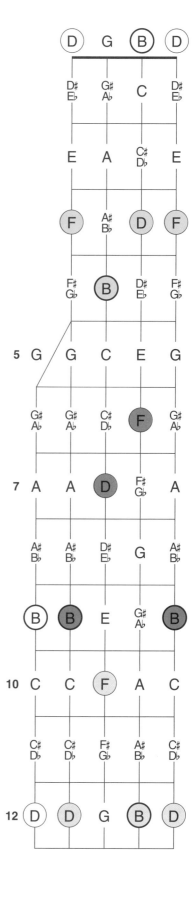

CHORDS

TRIADS WITH ADDED NOTES

Cadd9

C–E–G–D

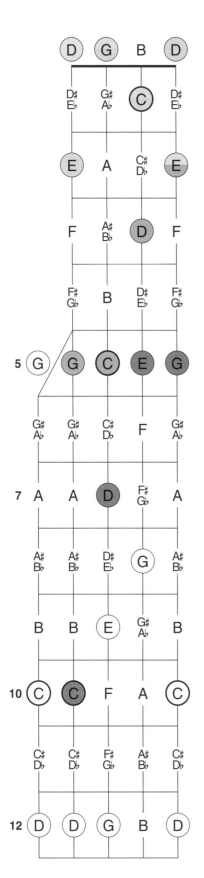

C♯/D♭add9

C♯–E♯–G♯–D♯/D♭–F–A♭–E♭

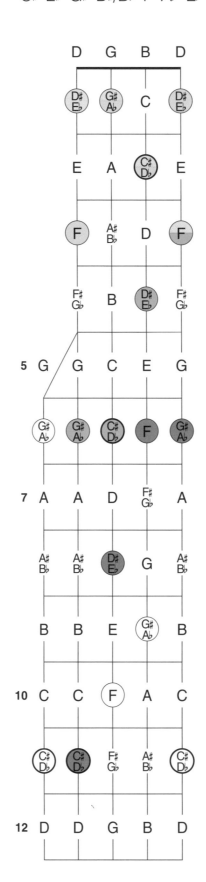

Dadd9

D–F♯–A–E

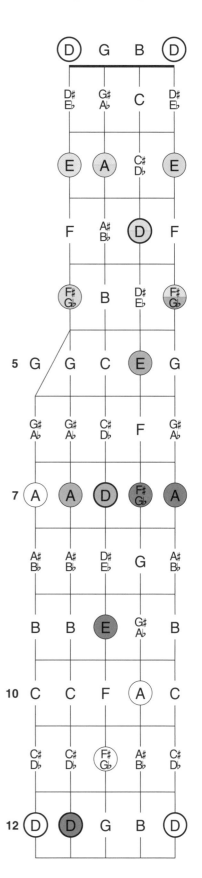

E♭add9

E♭–G–B♭–F

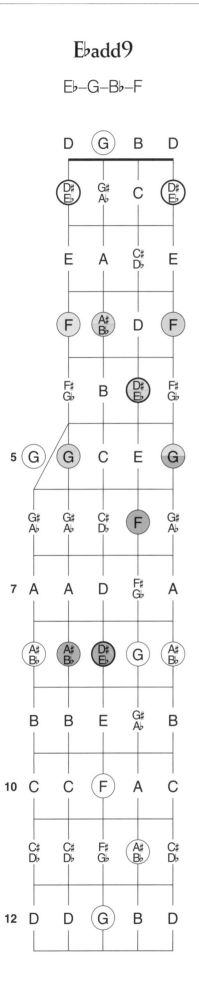

Eadd9

E–G♯–B–F♯

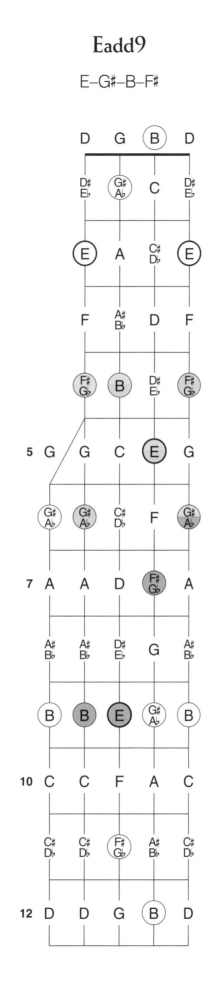

Fadd9

F–A–C–G

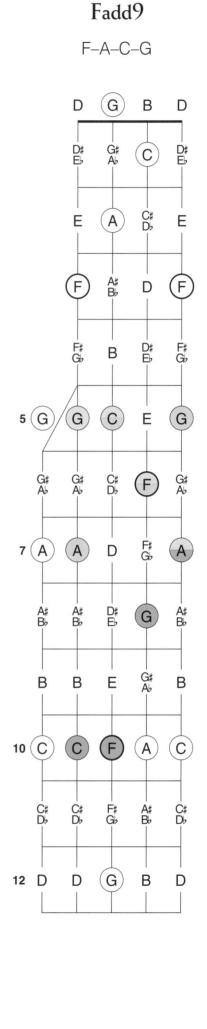

F#/G♭add9

F#–A#–C#–G#/G♭–B♭–D♭–A♭

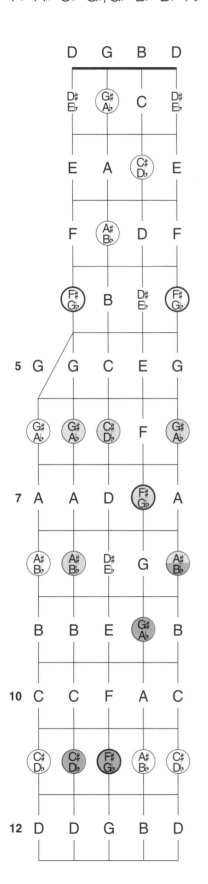

Gadd9

G–B–D–A

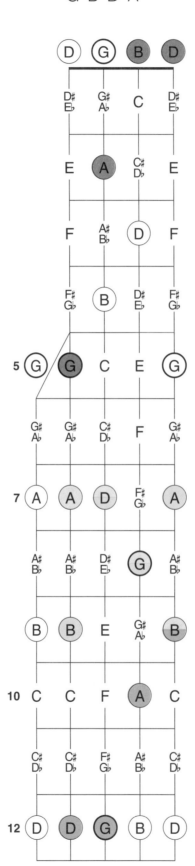

A♭add9

A♭–C–E♭–B♭

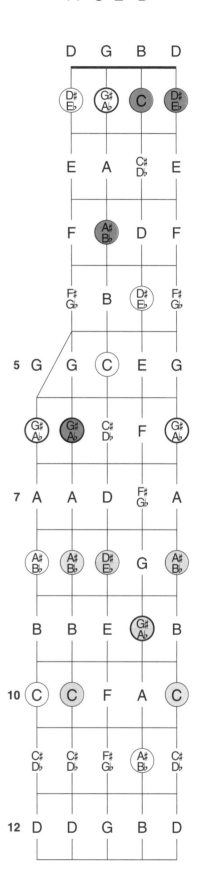

Aadd9

A–C#–E–B

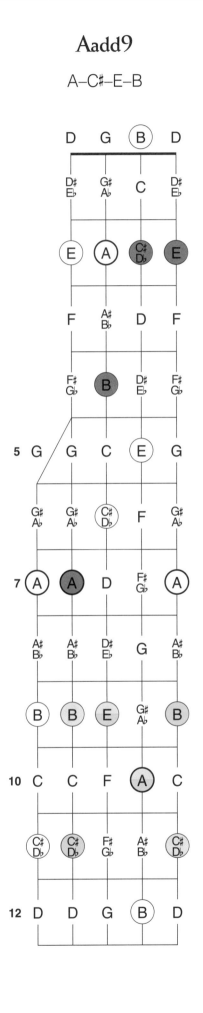

B♭add9

B♭–D–F–C

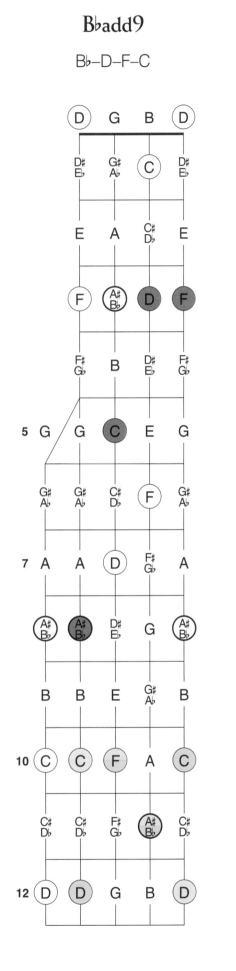

Badd9

B–D#–F#–C#

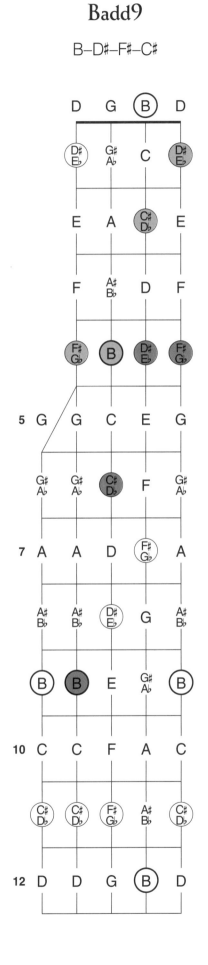

Cm(add9)

C–E♭–G–D

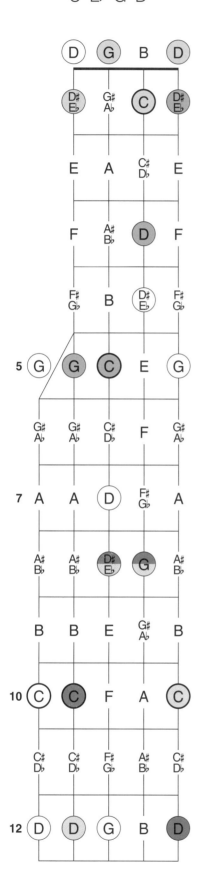

C♯m(add9)

C♯–E–G♯–D♯

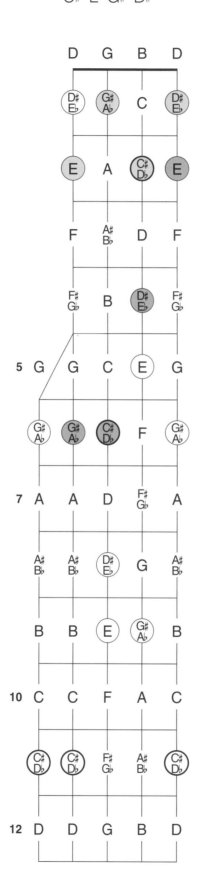

Dm(add9)

D–F–A–E

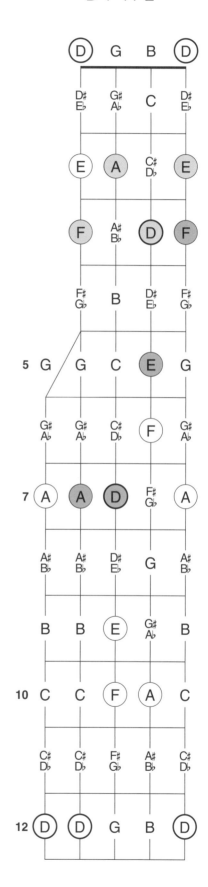

E♭m(add9)

E♭–G♭–B♭–F

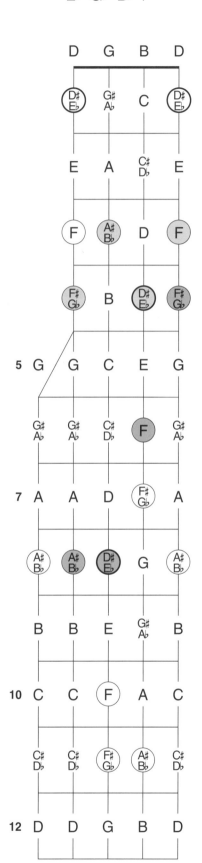

Em(add9)

E–G–B–F♯

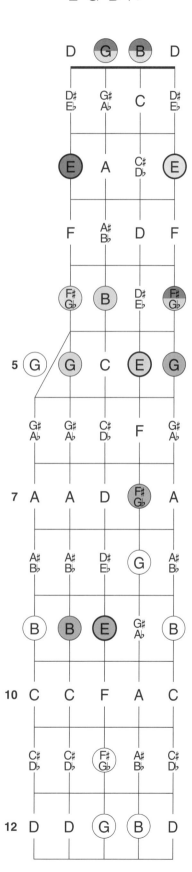

Fm(add9)

F–A♭–C–G

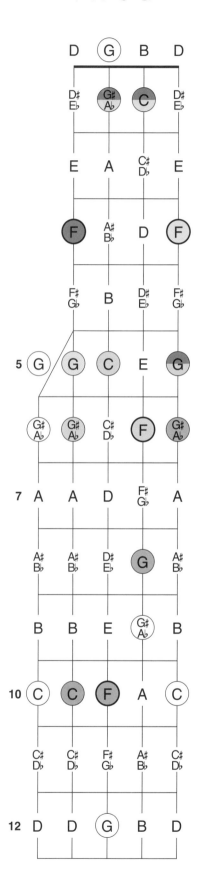

F#m(add9)

F#–A–C#–G#

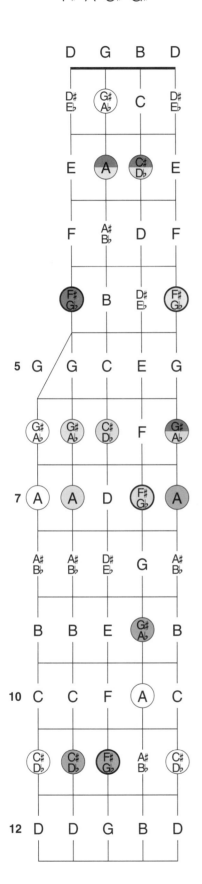

Gm(add9)

G–B♭–D–A

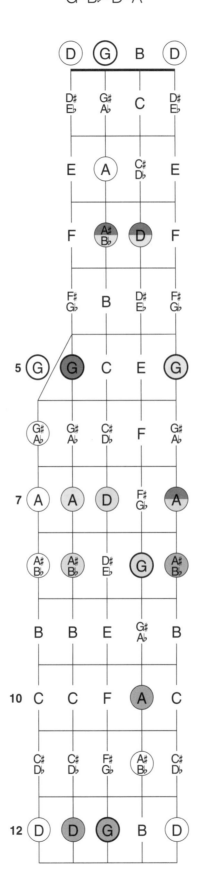

G#/A♭m(add9)

G#–B–D#–A#/A♭–C♭–E♭–B♭

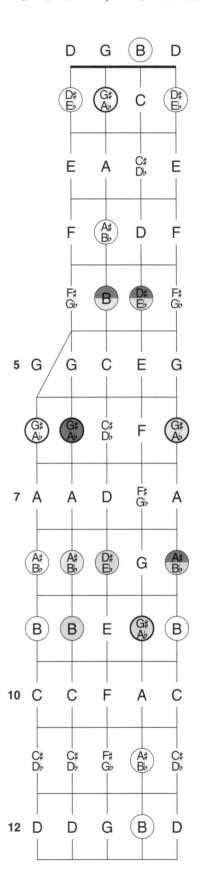

Am(add9)

A–C–E–B

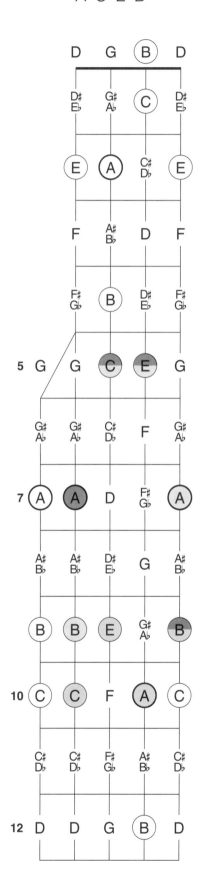

B♭m(add9)

B♭–D♭–F–C

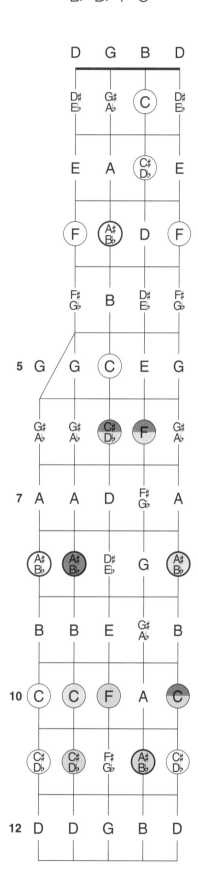

Bm(add9)

B–D–F♯–C♯

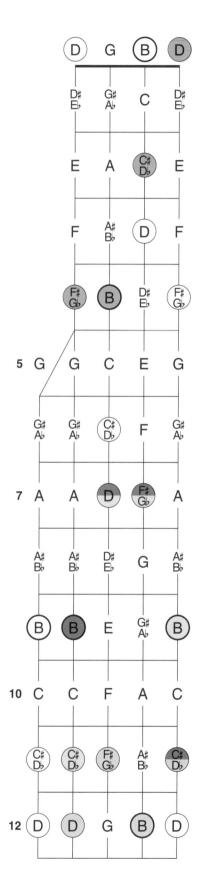

C6

C–E–G–A

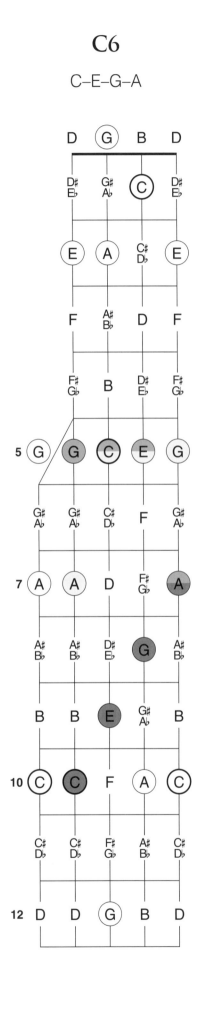

C#/Db6

C#–E#–G#–A#/Db–F–Ab–Bb

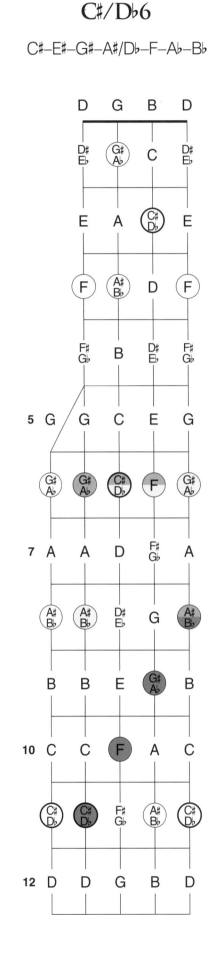

D6

D–F#–A–B

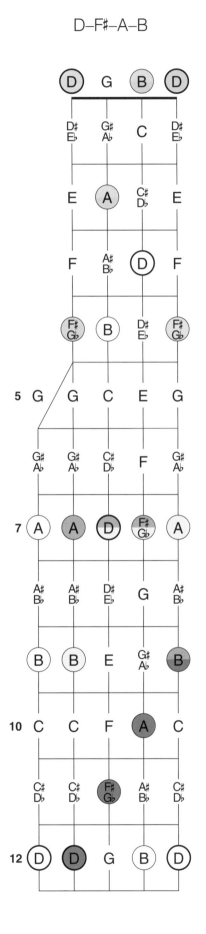

E♭6

Eb–G–Bb–C

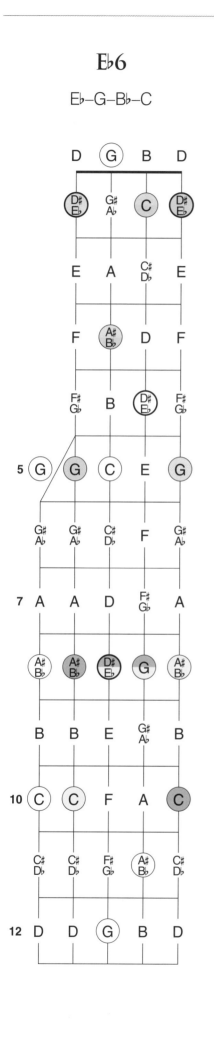

E6

E–G#–B–C#

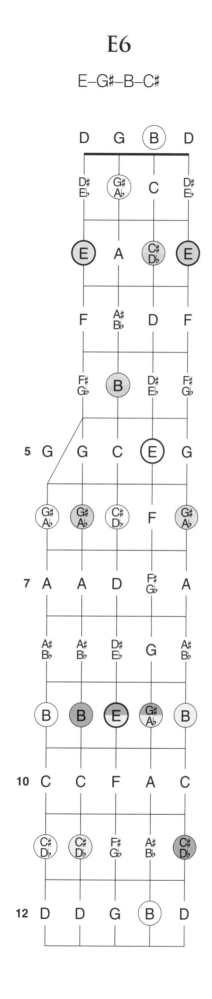

F6

F–A–C–D

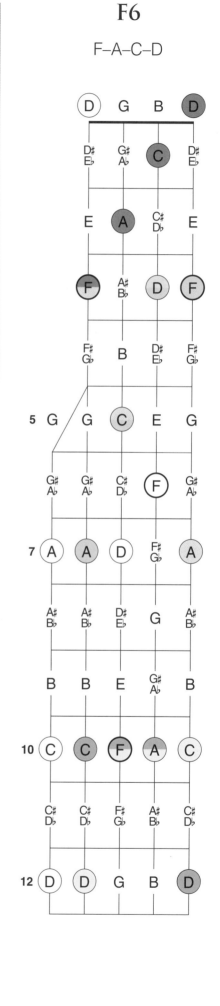

F#/G♭6

F#–A#–C#–D#/G♭–B♭–D♭–E♭

G6

G–B–D–E

A♭6

A♭–C–E♭–F

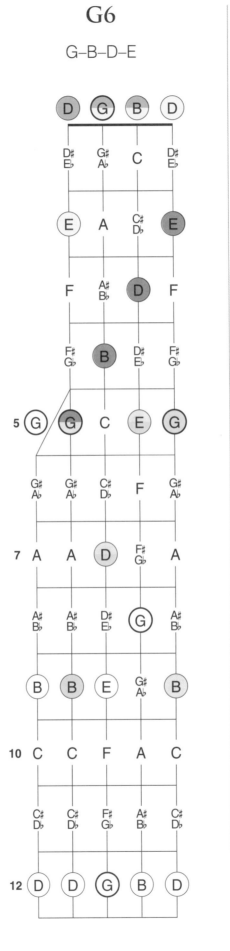
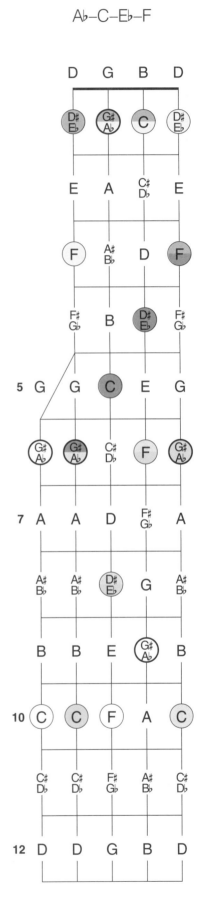

A6

A–C#–E–F#

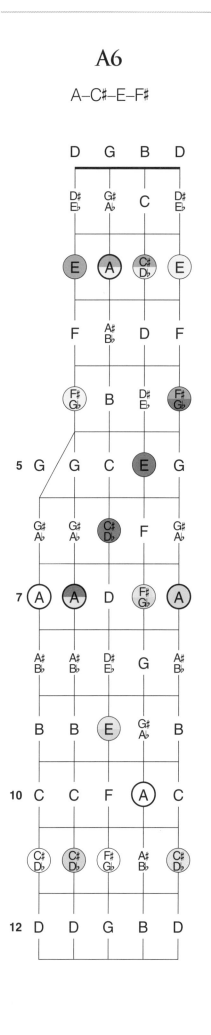

B♭6

B♭–D–F–G

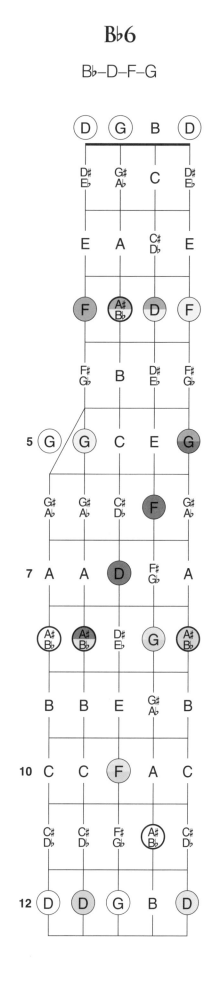

B6

B–D#–F#–G#

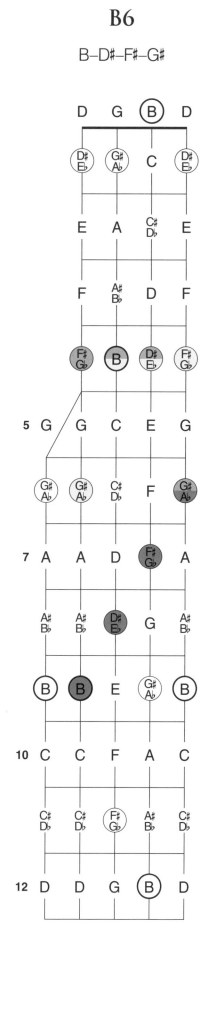

Cm6

C–E♭–G–A

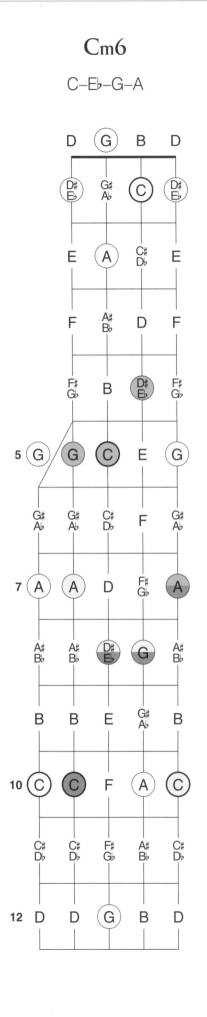

C#m6

C#–E–G#–A#

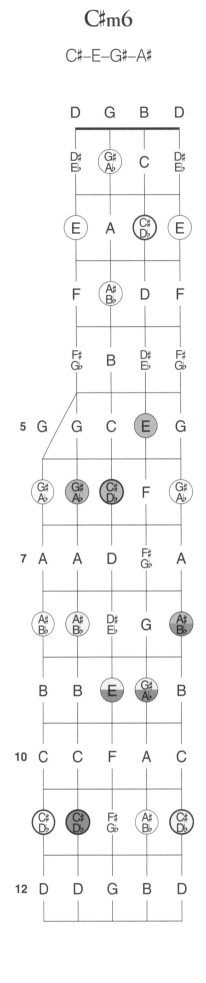

Dm6

D–F–A–B

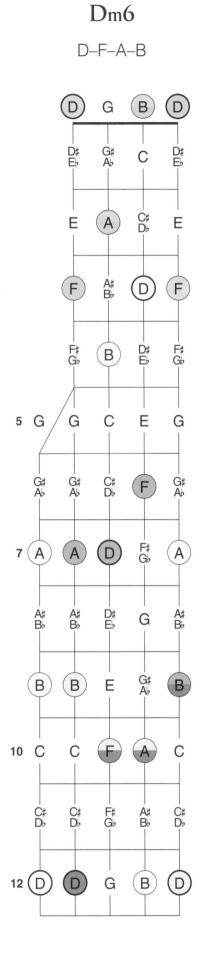

Ebm6

Eb–Gb–Bb–C

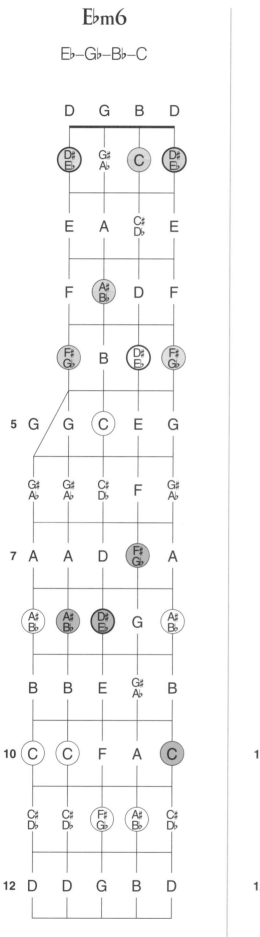

Em6

E–G–B–C#

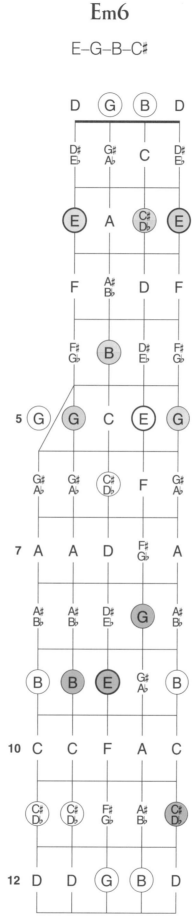

Fm6

F–Ab–C–D

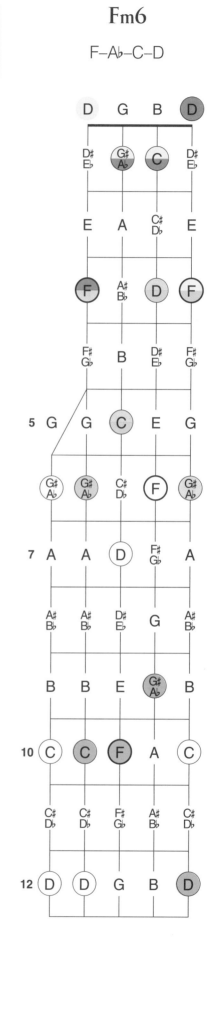

F#m6

F#–A–C#–D#

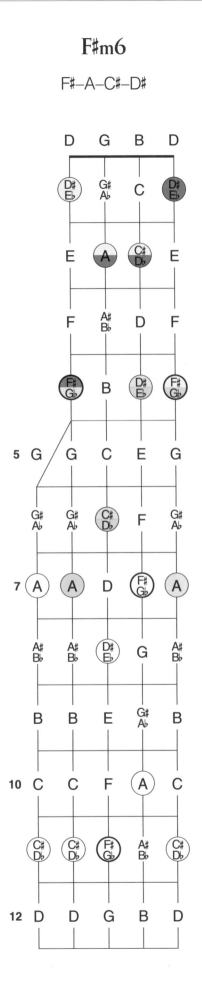

Gm6

G–Bb–D–E

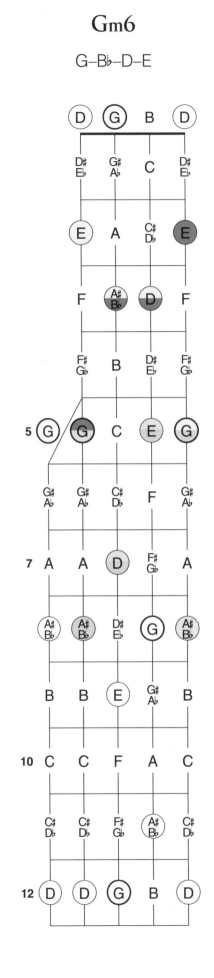

Abm6

Ab–Cb–Eb–F

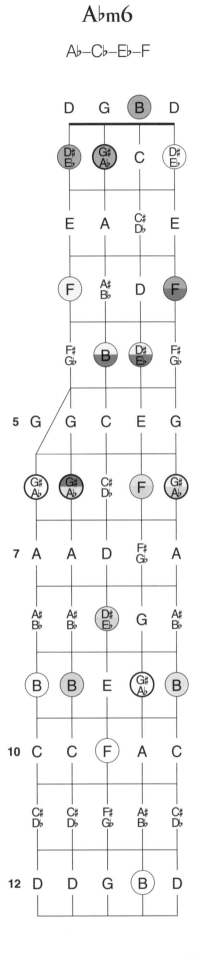

Am6

A–C–E–F#

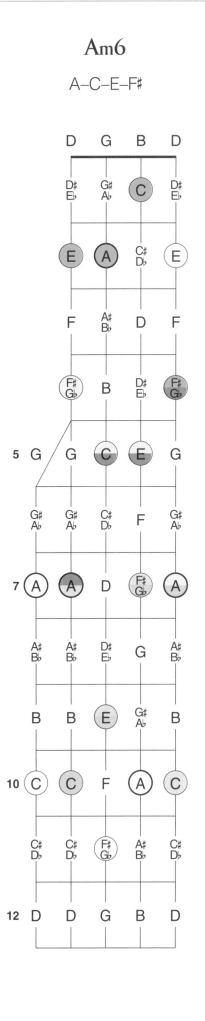

B♭m6

B♭–D♭–F–G

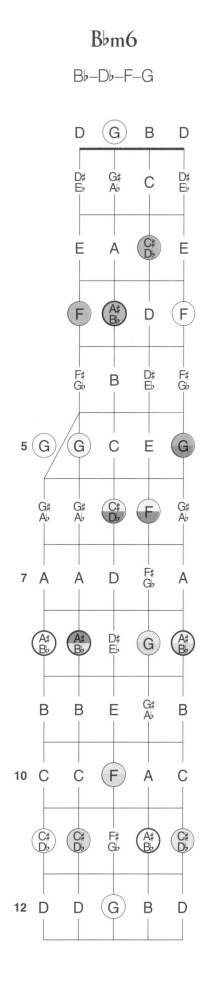

Bm6

B–D–F#–G#

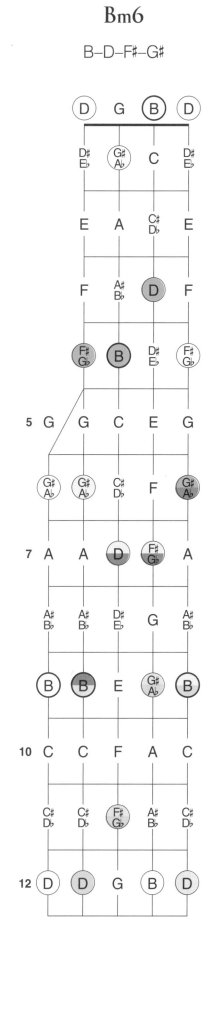

C$^6_9$

C–E–G–A–D

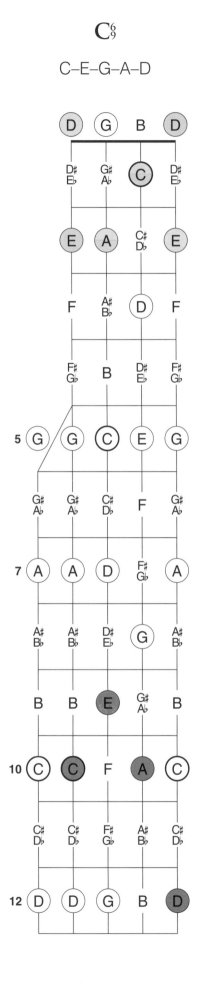

C#/D♭$^6_9$

C#–E#–G#–A#–D#/D♭–F–A♭–B♭–E♭

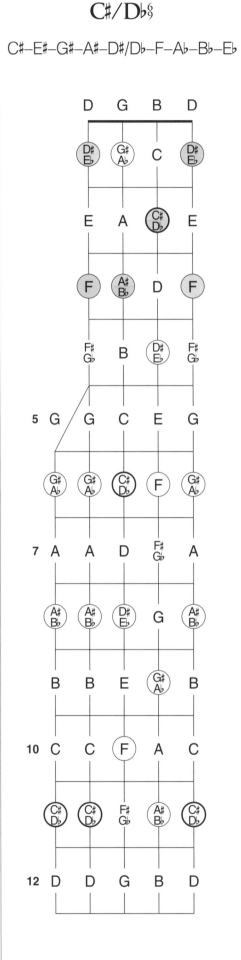

D$^6_9$

D–F#–A–B–E

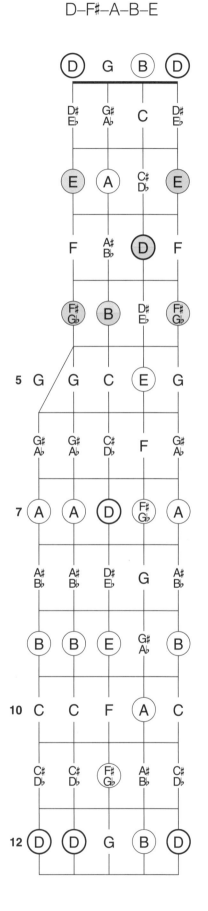

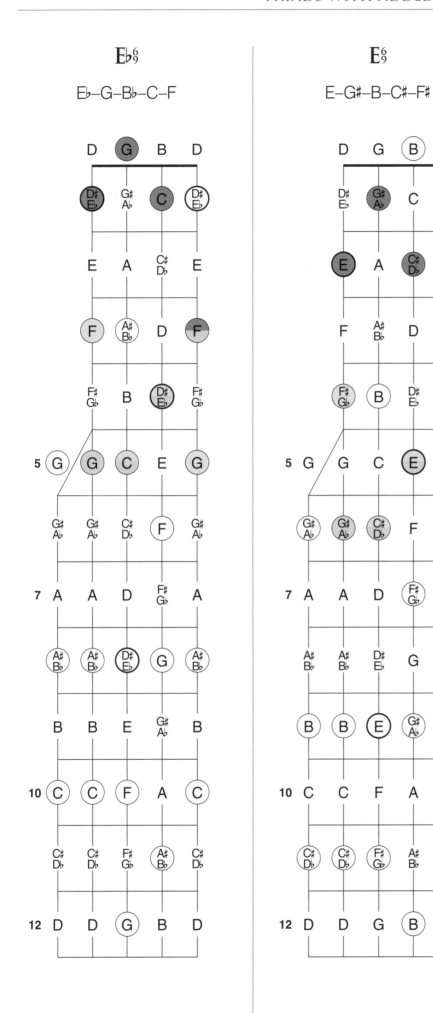

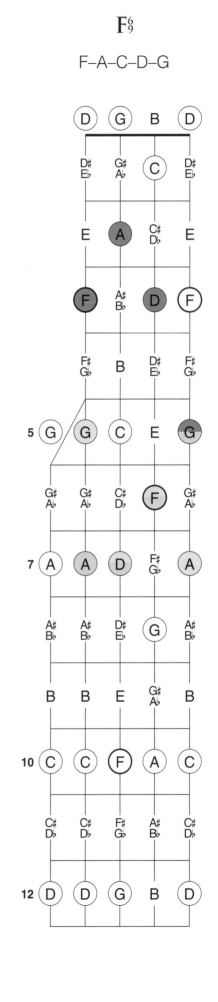

F#/Gb⁶₉

F#–A#–C#–D#–G#/Gb–Bb–Db–Eb–Ab

G⁶₉

G–B–D–E–A

Ab⁶₉

Ab–C–Eb–F–Bb

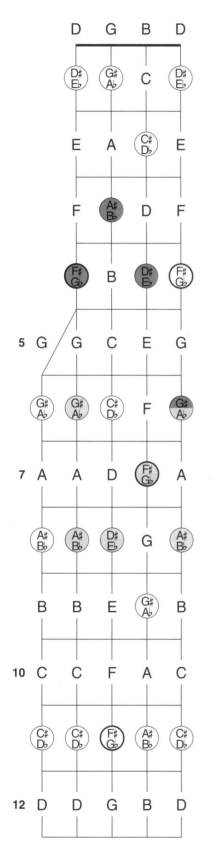

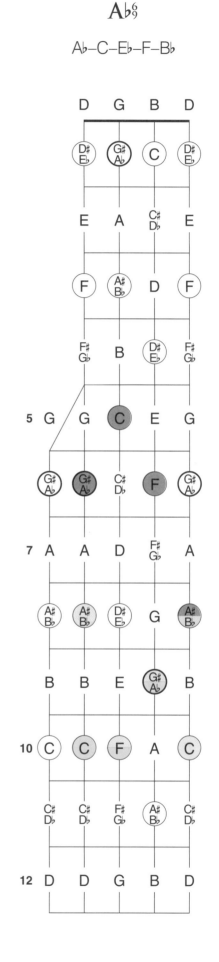

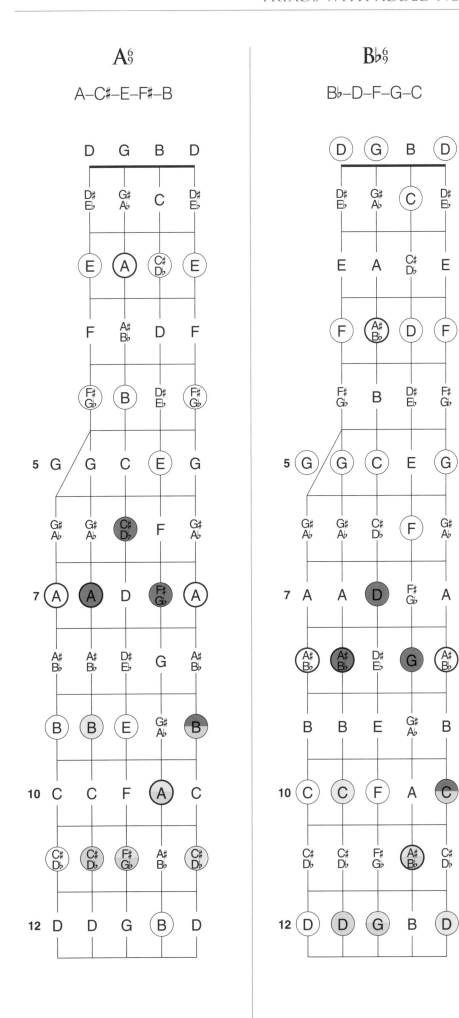

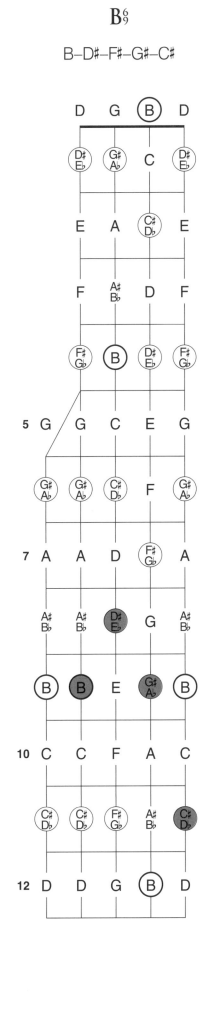

Cm$_9^6$

C–E♭–G–A–D

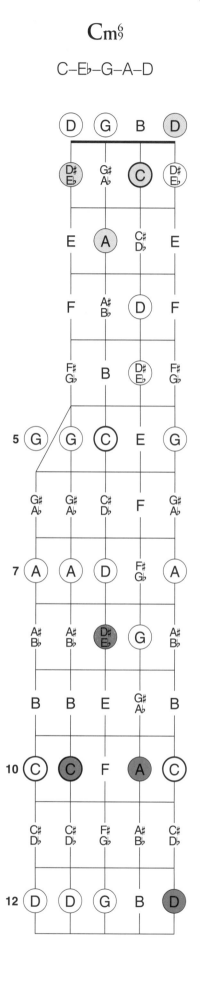

C♯m$_9^6$

C♯–E–G♯–A♯–D♯

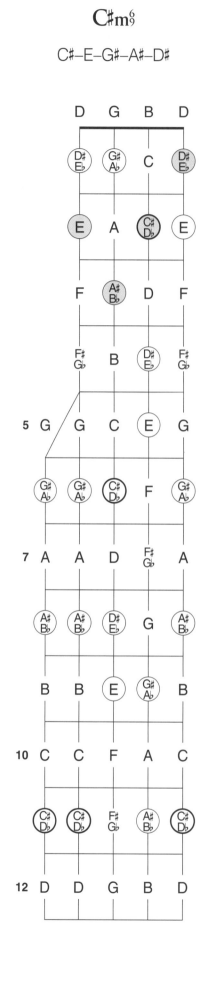

Dm$_9^6$

D–F–A–B–E

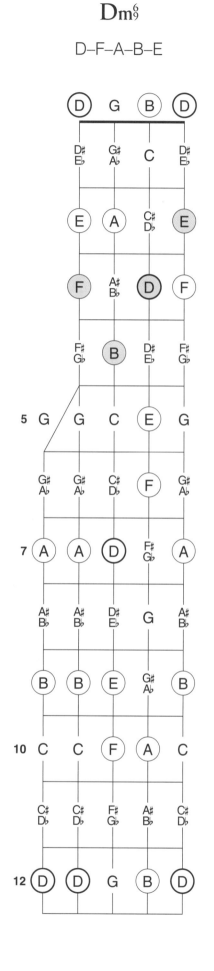

E♭m⁶₉

E♭–G♭–B♭–C–F

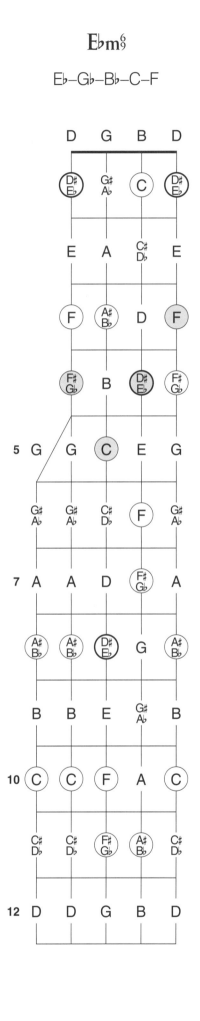

Em⁶₉

E–G–B–C♯–F♯

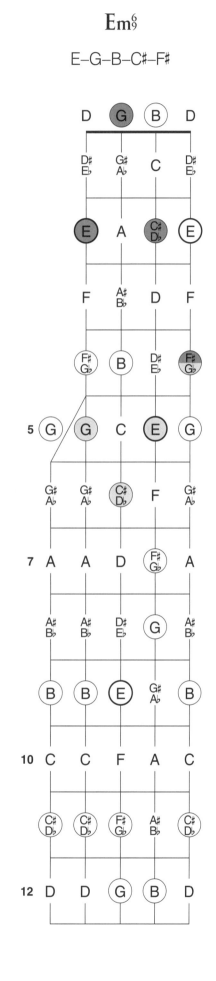

Fm⁶₉

F–A♭–C–D–G

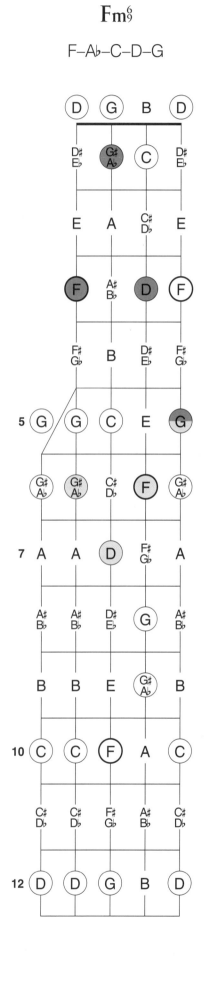

F#m⁶

F#–A–C#–D#–G#

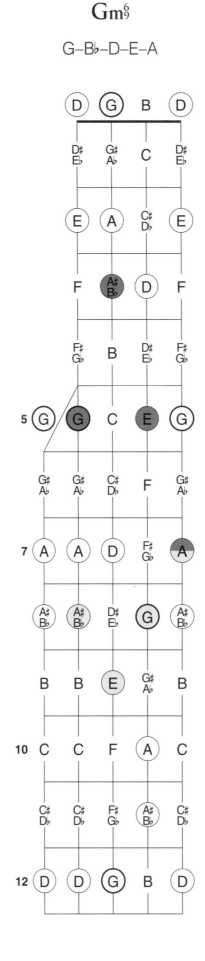

Gm⁶

G–B♭–D–E–A

A♭m⁶

A♭–C♭–E♭–F–B♭

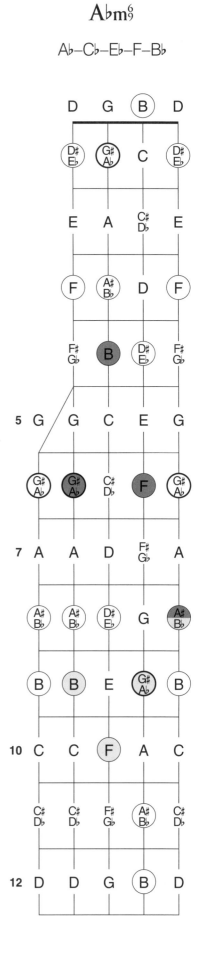

Am⁶₉

A–C–E–F♯–B

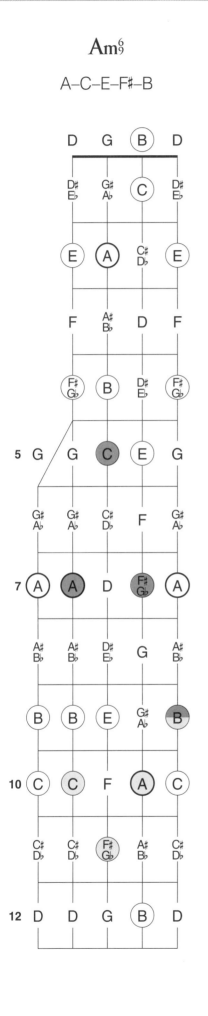

B♭m⁶₉

B♭–D♭–F–G–C

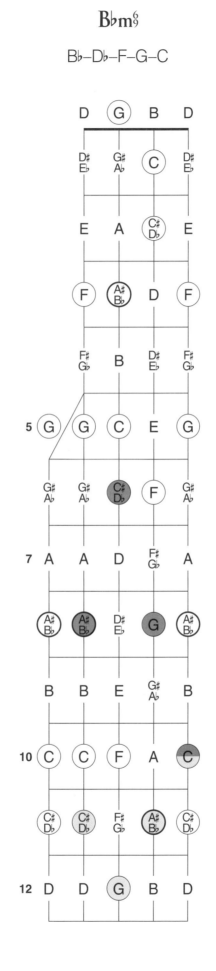

Bm⁶₉

B–D–F♯–G♯–C♯

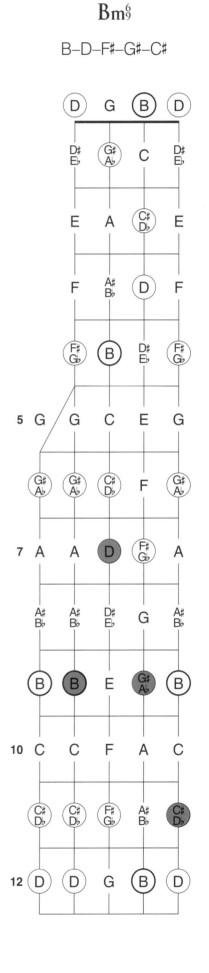

127

CHORDS

SEVENTH CHORDS

Cmaj7

C–E–G–B

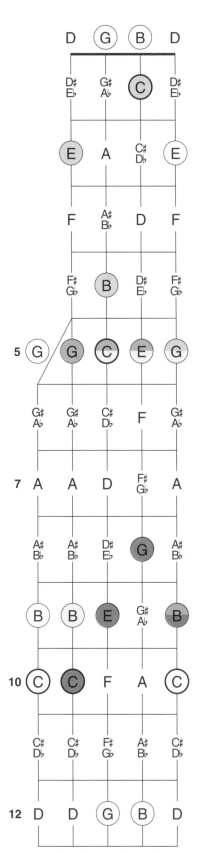

C#/D♭maj7

C#–E#–G#–B#/D♭–F–A♭–C

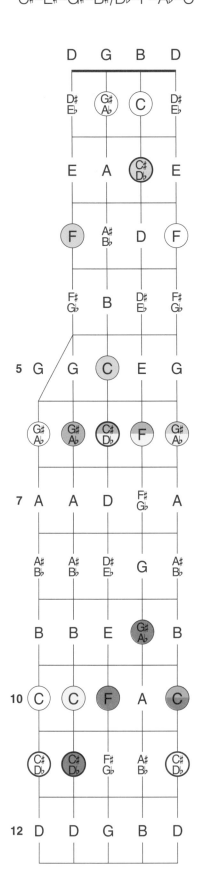

Dmaj7

D–F#–A–C#

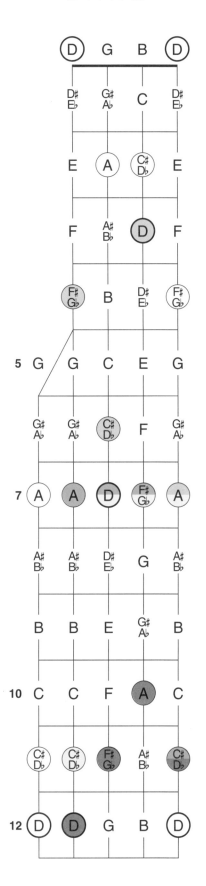

E♭maj7

E♭–G–B♭–D

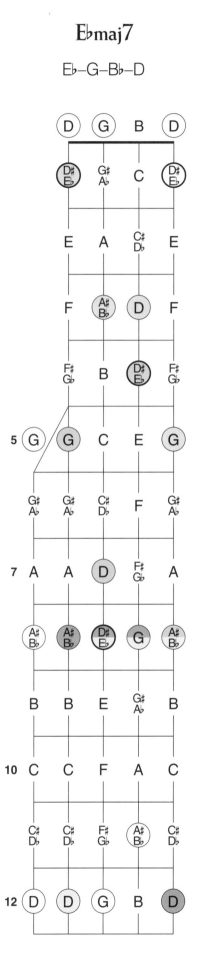

Emaj7

E–G♯–B–D♯

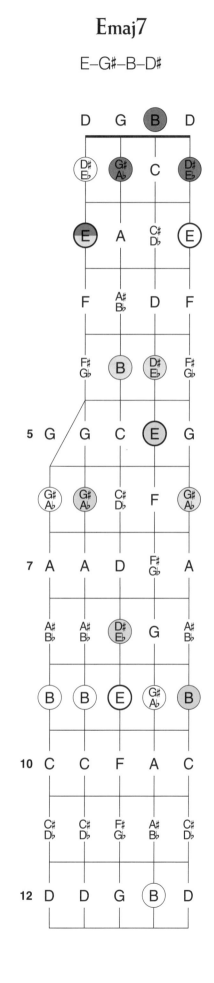

Fmaj7

F–A–C–E

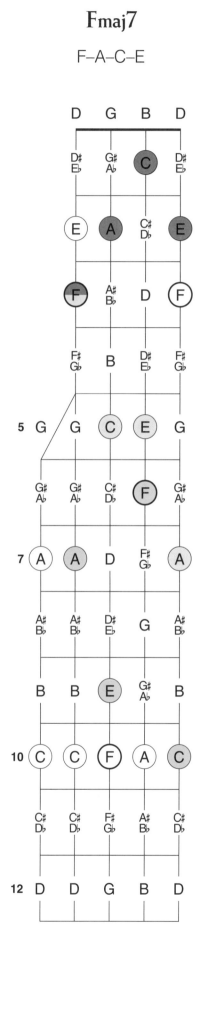

F#/G♭maj7

F#–A#–C#–E#/G♭–B♭–D♭–F

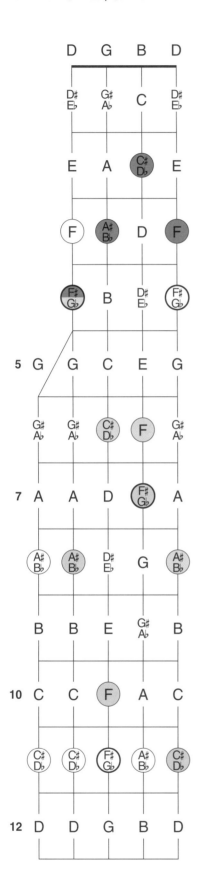

Gmaj7

G–B–D–F#

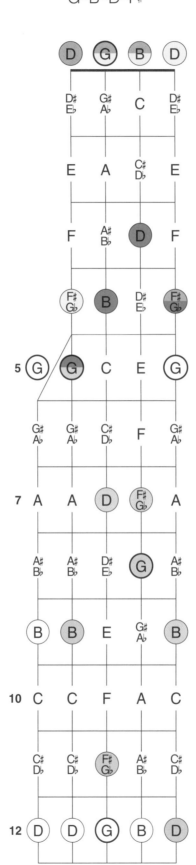

A♭maj7

A♭–C–E♭–G

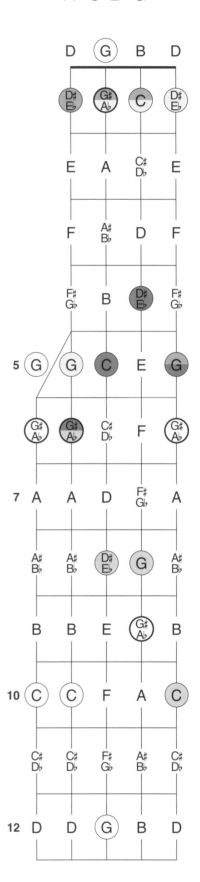

Amaj7

A–C#–E–G#

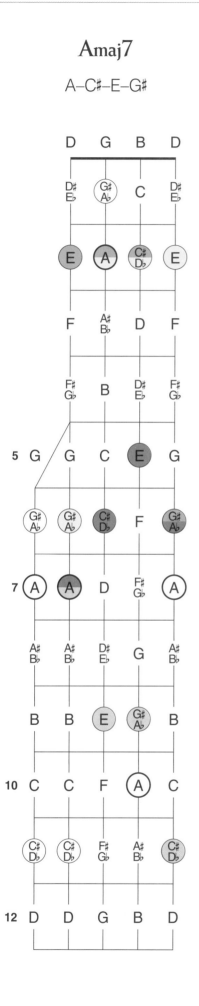

B♭maj7

B♭–D–F–A

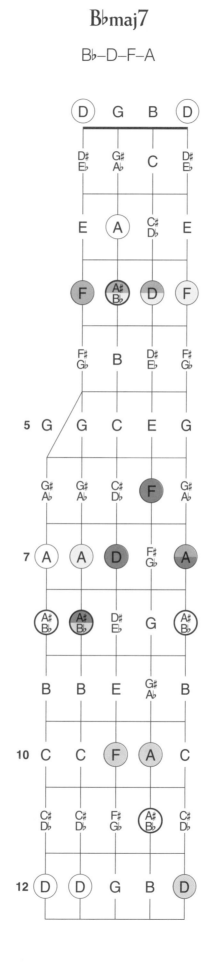

Bmaj7

B–D#–F#–A#

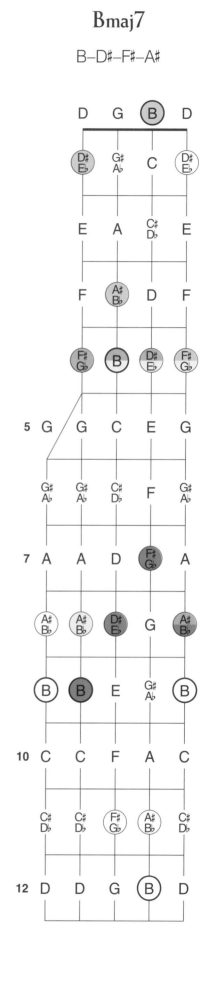

C7

C–E–G–B♭

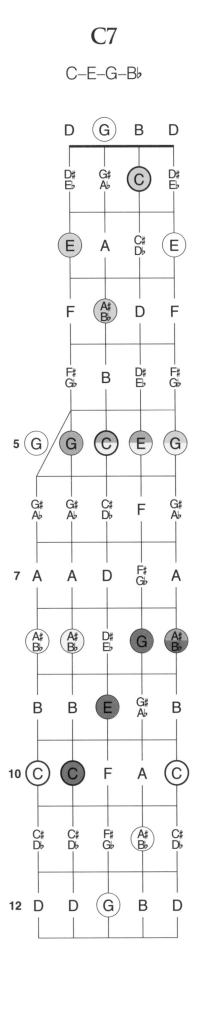

C♯/D♭7

C♯–E♯–G♯–B/D♭–F–A♭–C♭

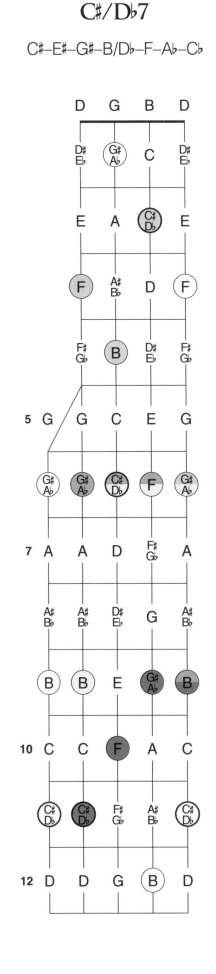

D7

D–F♯–A–C

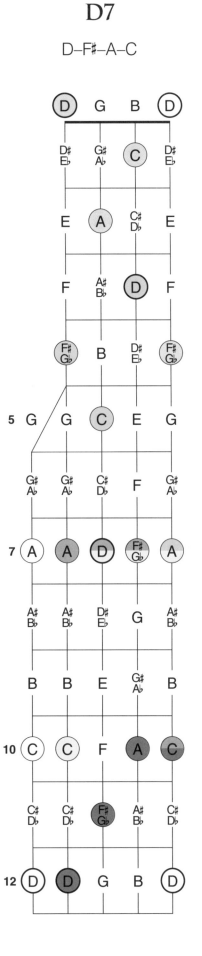

E♭7

E♭–G–B♭–D♭

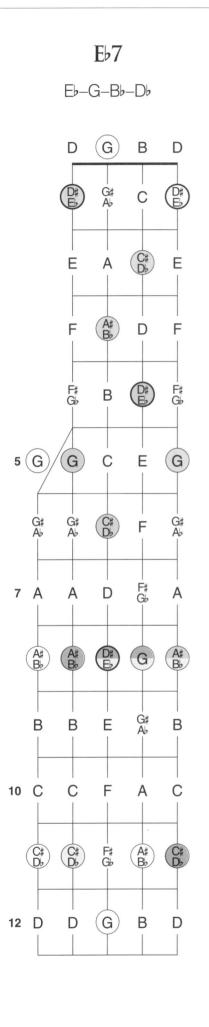

E7

E–G#–B–D

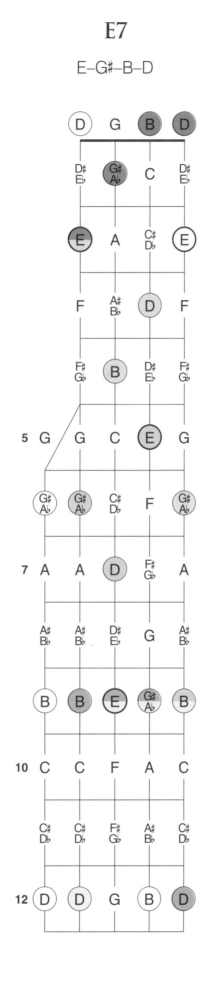

F7

F–A–C–E♭

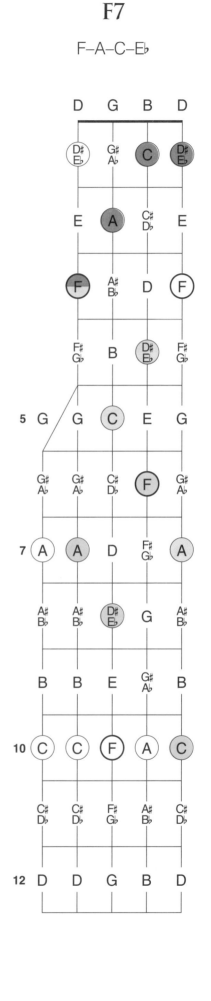

F#/Gb7

F#–A#–C#–E/Gb–Bb–Db–Fb

G7

G–B–D–F

Ab7

Ab–C–Eb–Gb

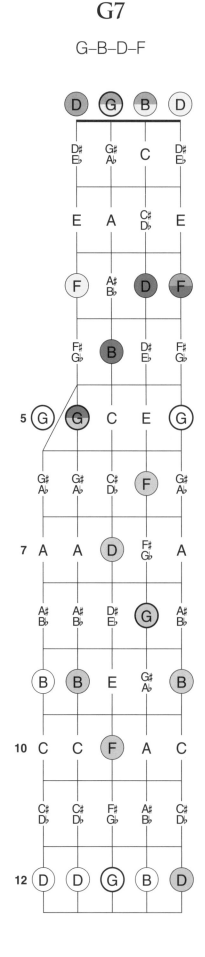

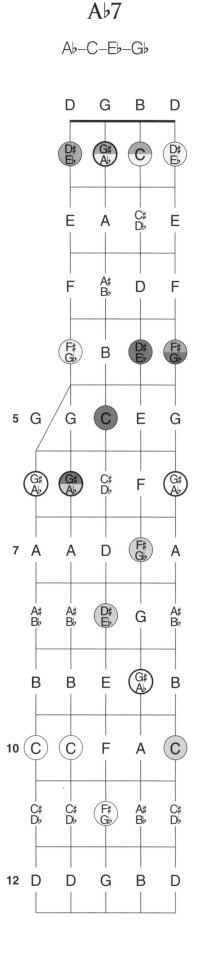

A7

A–C#–E–G

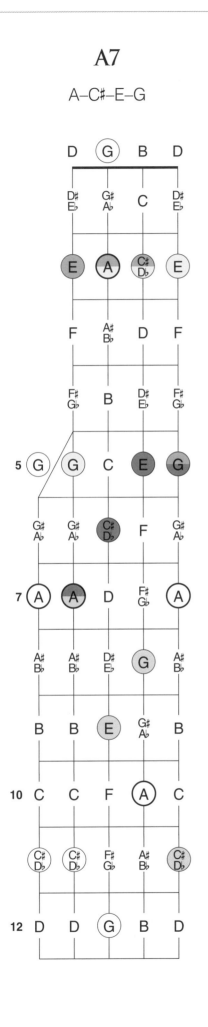

B♭7

B♭–D–F–A♭

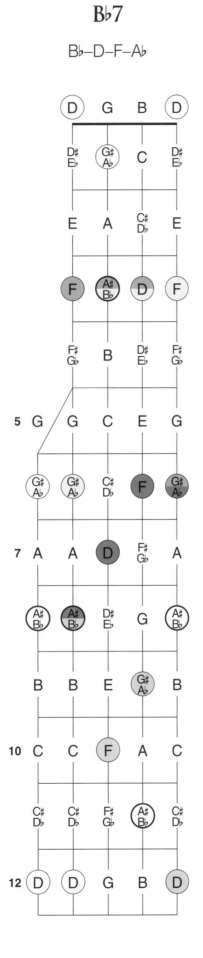

B7

B–D#–F#–A

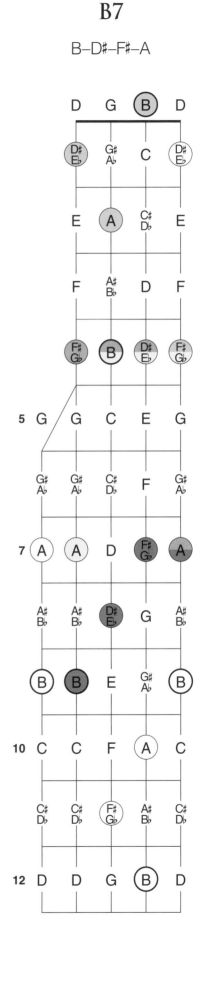

C7sus4

C–F–G–Bb

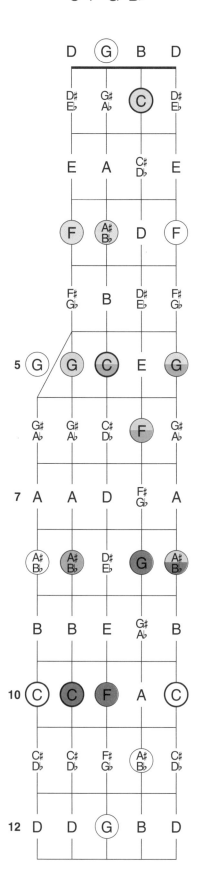

C#/Db7sus4

C#–F#–G#–B/Db–Gb–Ab–Cb

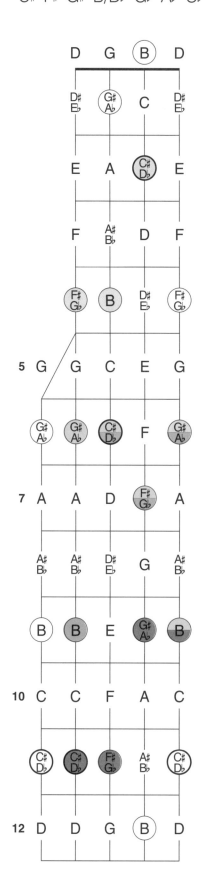

D7sus4

D–G–A–C

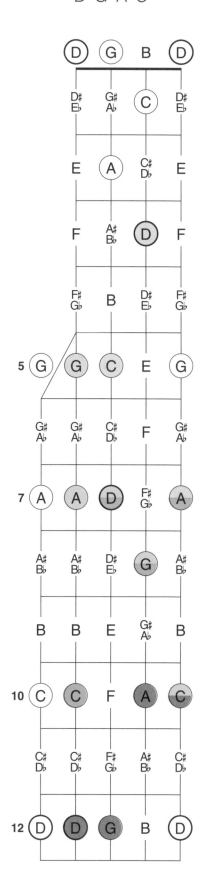

Eb7sus4

Eb–Ab–Bb–Db

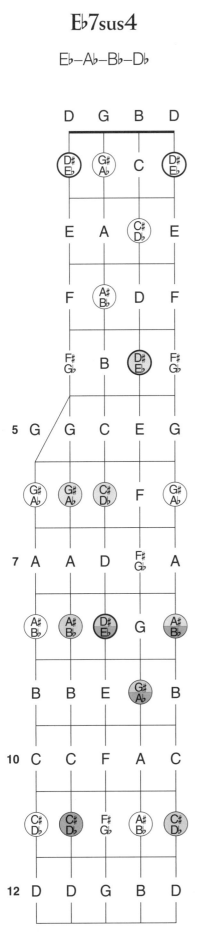

E7sus4

E–A–B–D

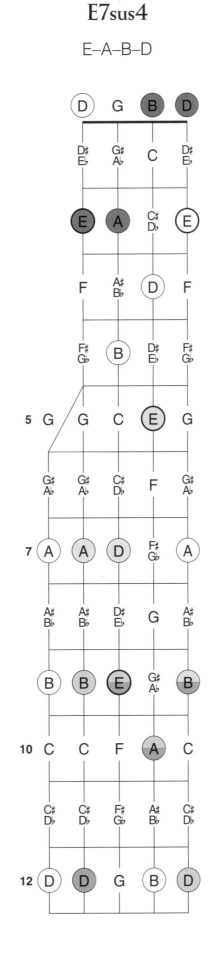

F7sus4

F–Bb–C–Eb

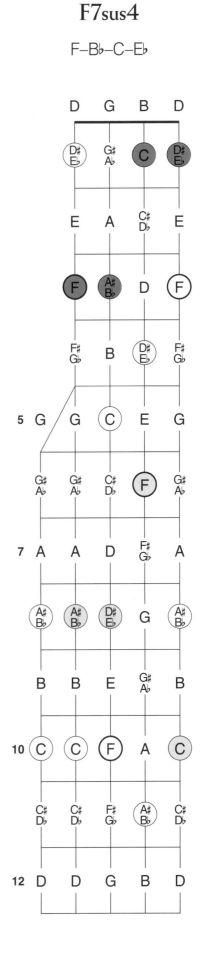

F#7sus4

F#–B–C#–E

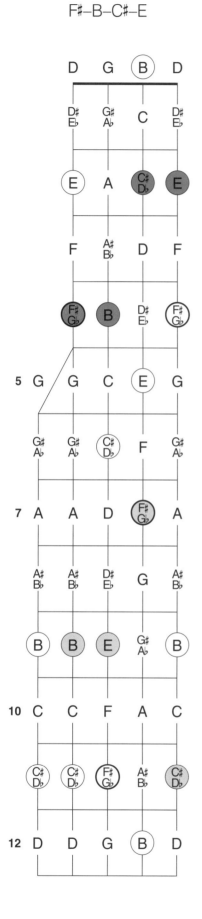

G7sus4

G–C–D–F

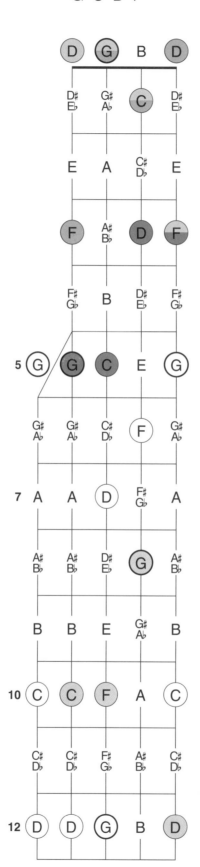

Ab7sus4

Ab–Db–Eb–Gb

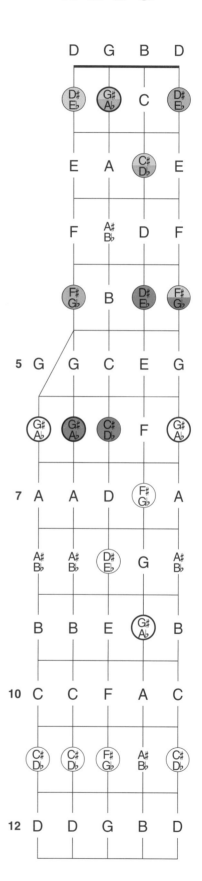

A7sus4

A–D–E–G

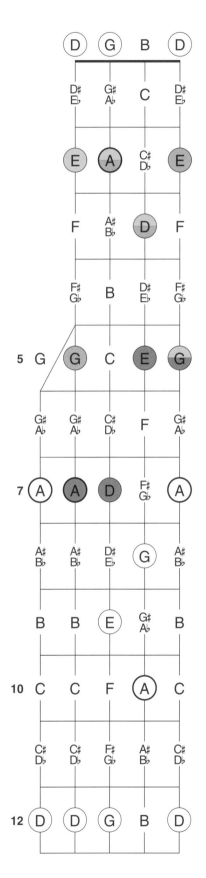

B♭7sus4

B♭–E♭–F–A♭

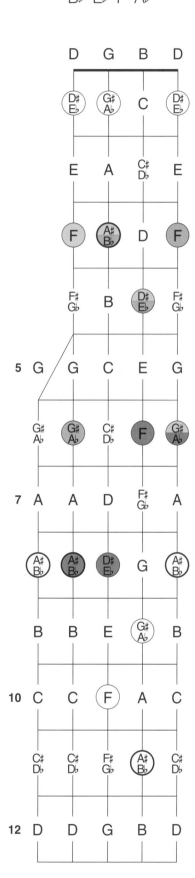

B7sus4

B–E–F♯–A

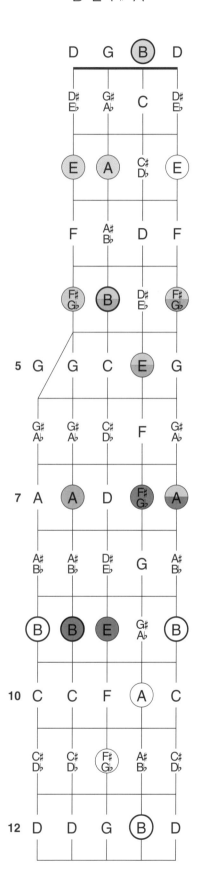

Cm7

C–E♭–G–B♭

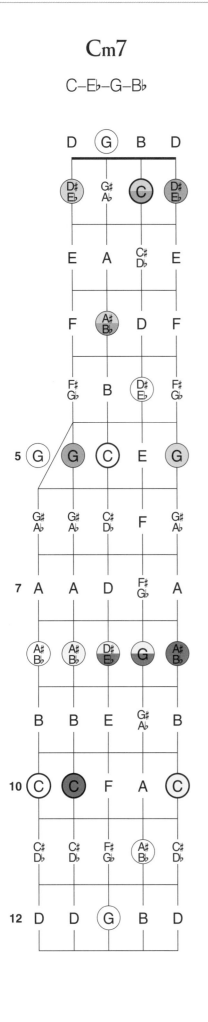

C♯m7

C♯–E–G♯–B

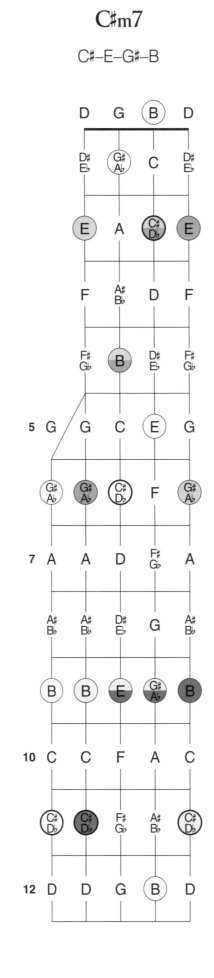

Dm7

D–F–A–C

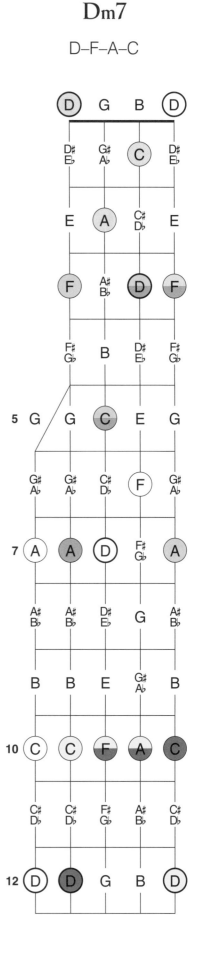

D#/E♭m7

D#–F#–A#–C#/E♭–G♭–B♭–D♭

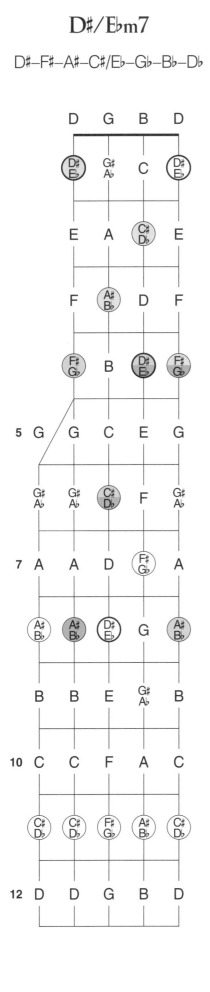

Em7

E–G–B–D

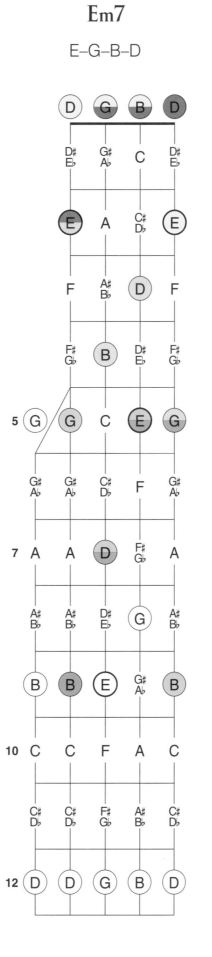

Fm7

F–A♭–C–E♭

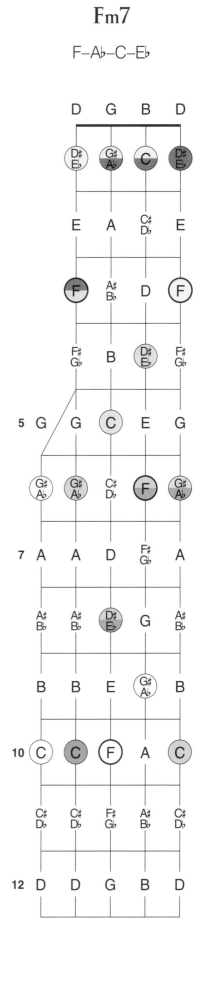

F#m7

F#–A–C#–E

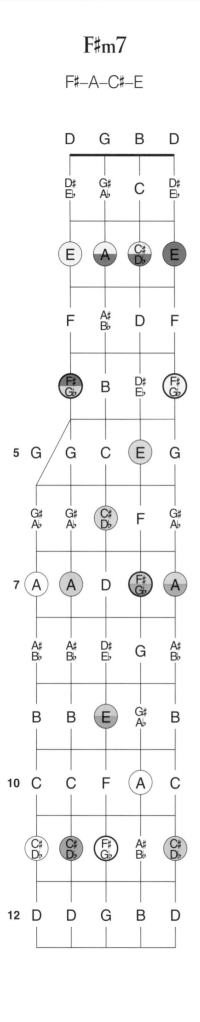

Gm7

G–Bb–D–F

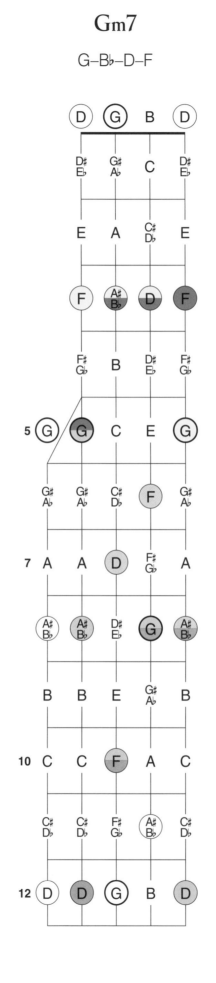

Abm7

Ab–Cb–Eb–Gb

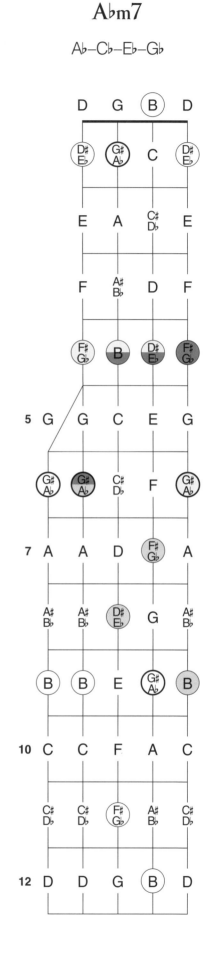

Am7

A–C–E–G

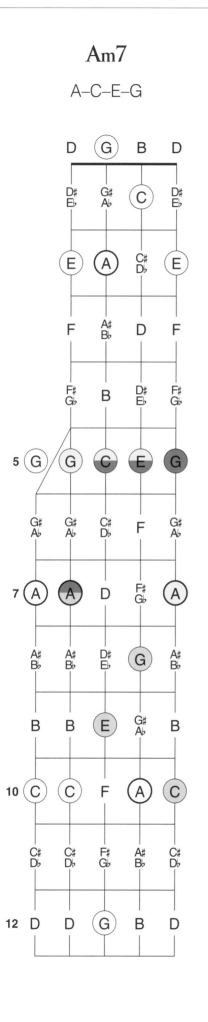

B♭m7

B♭–D♭–F–A♭

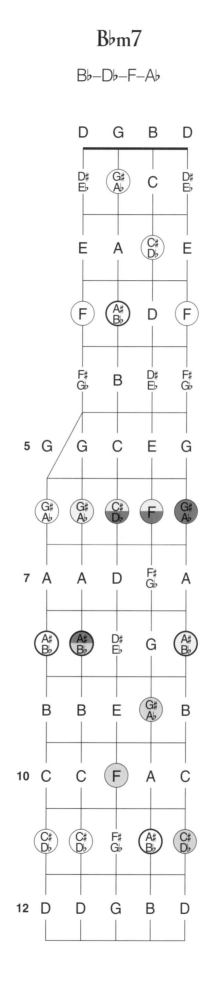

Bm7

B–D–F♯–A

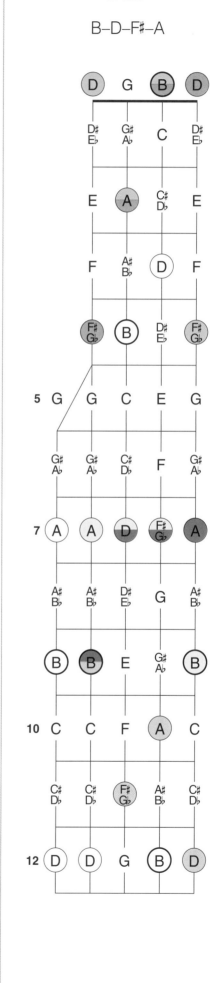

Cm(maj7)

C–E♭–G–B

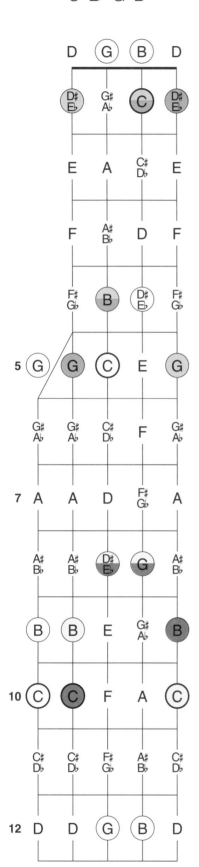

C#m(maj7)

C#–E–G#–B#

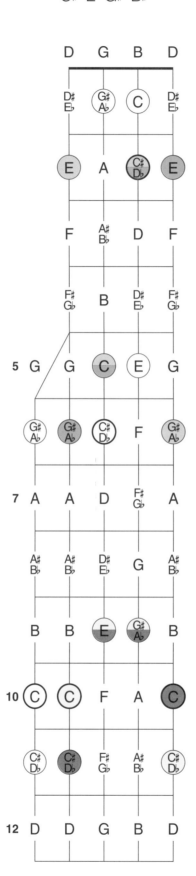

Dm(maj7)

D–F–A–C#

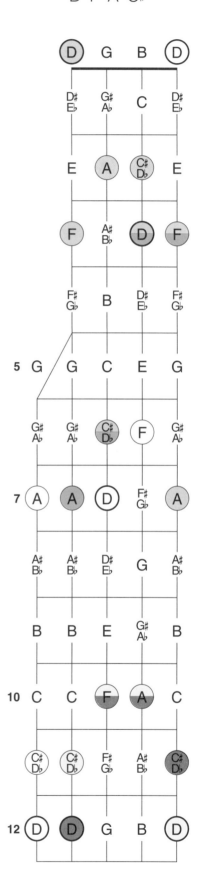

E♭m(maj7)
E♭–G♭–B♭–D

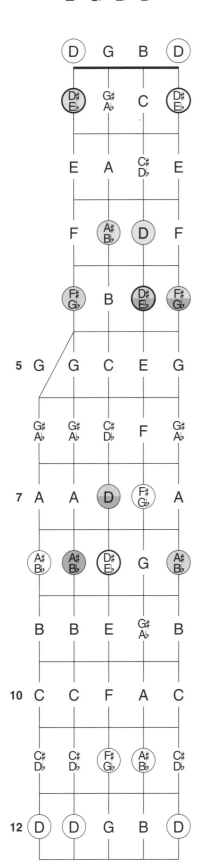

Em(maj7)
E–G–B–D♯

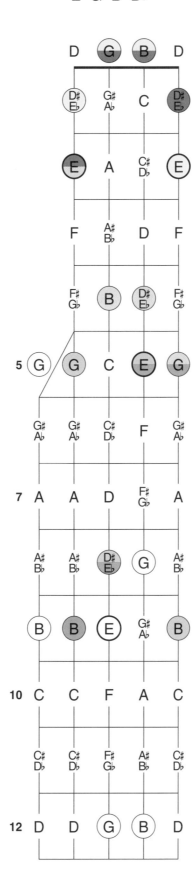

Fm(maj7)
F–A♭–C–E

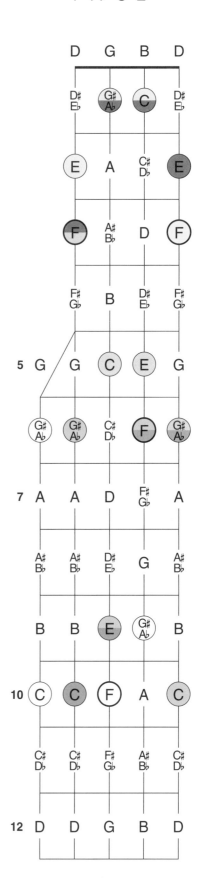

F#m(maj7)

F#–A–C#–E#

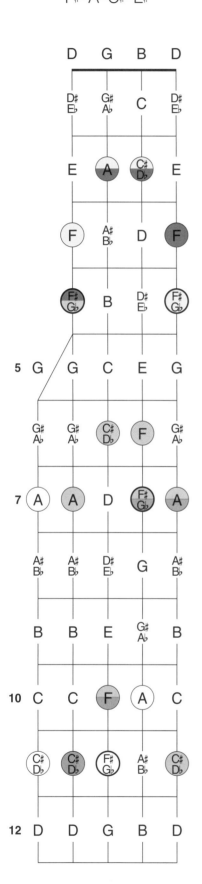

Gm(maj7)

G–B♭–D–F#

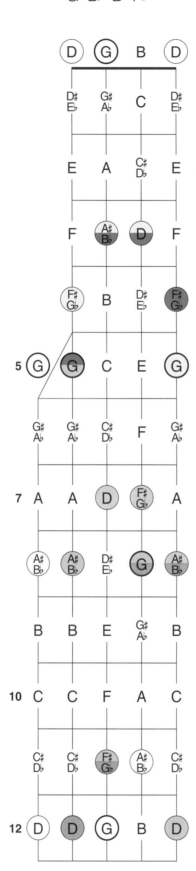

G#/A♭m(maj7)

G#–B–D#–F✕/A♭–C♭–E♭–G

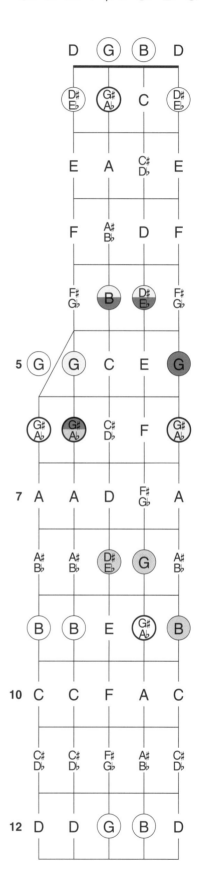

Am(maj7)

A–C–E–G♯

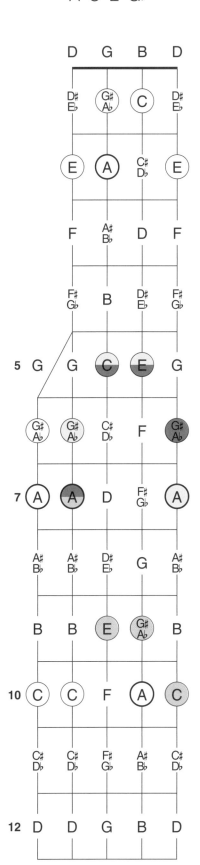

B♭m(maj7)

B♭–D♭–F–A

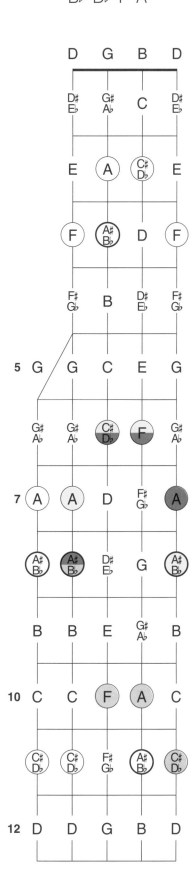

Bm(maj7)

B–D–F♯–A♯

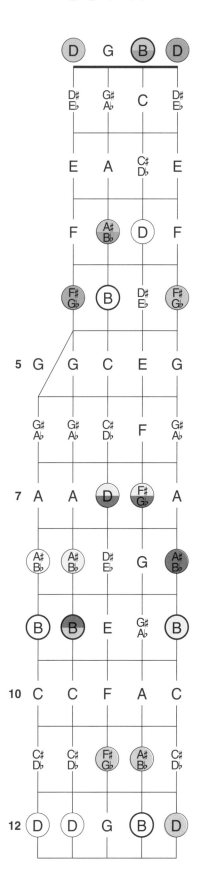

Cm7♭5

C–E♭–G♭–B♭

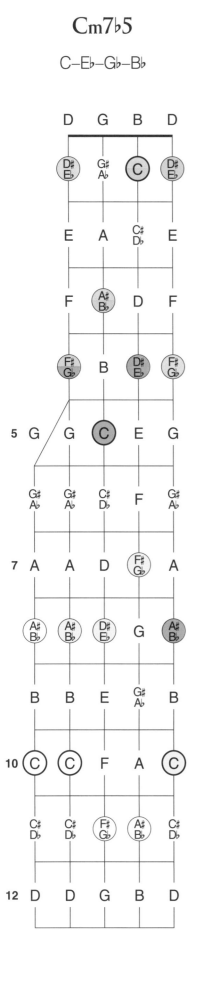

C#m7♭5

C#–E–G–B

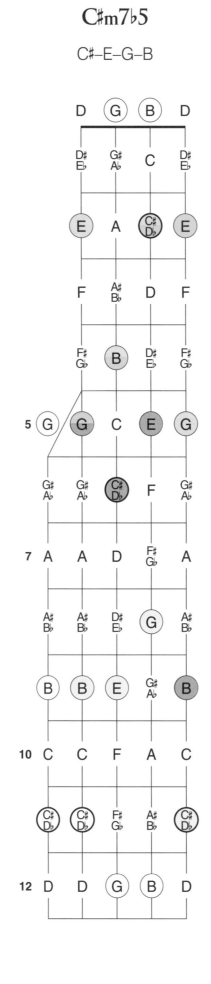

Dm7♭5

D–F–A♭–C

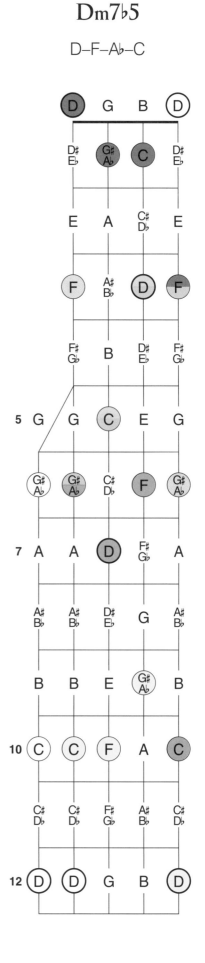

D#/E♭m7♭5

D#–F#–A–C#/E♭–G♭–B♭♭–D♭

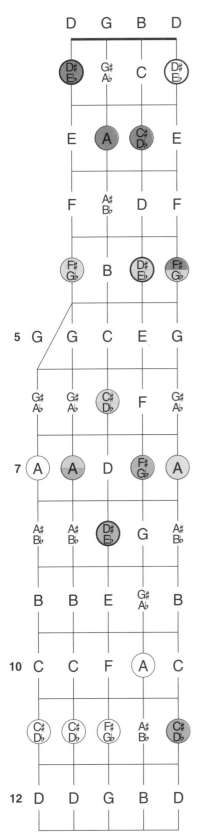

Em7♭5

E–G–B♭–D

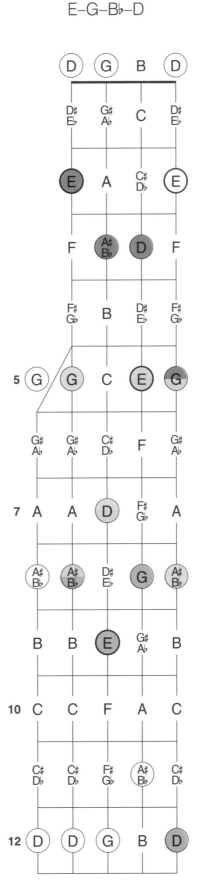

Fm7♭5

F–A♭–C♭–E♭

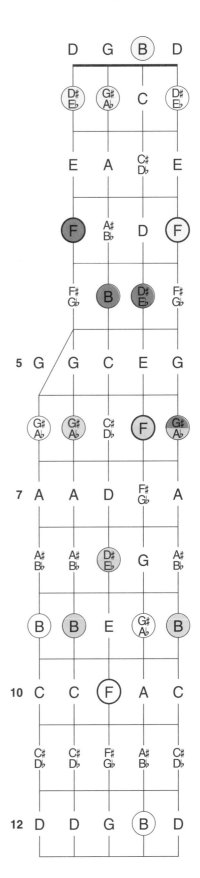

F#m7♭5

F#–A–C–E

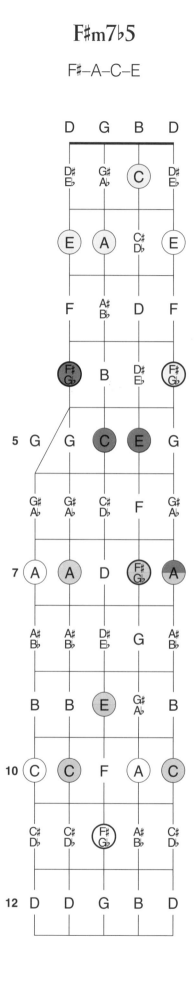

Gm7♭5

G–B♭–D♭–F

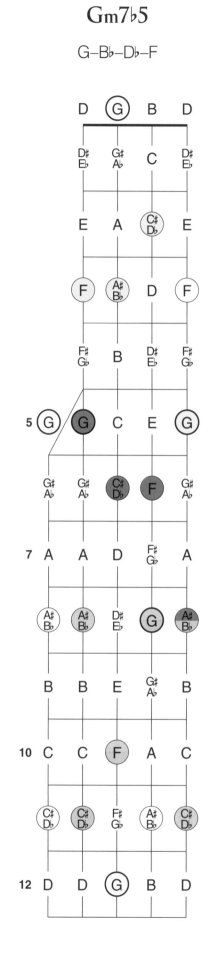

G#m7♭5

G#–B–D–F#

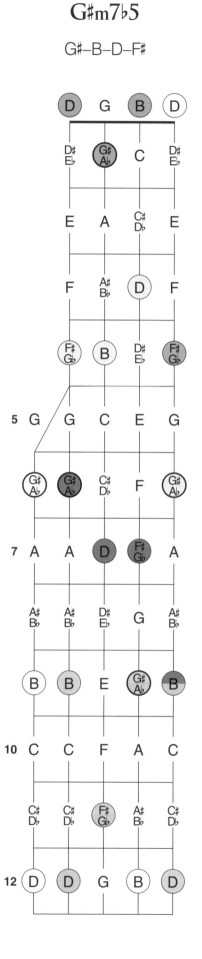

Am7♭5

A–C–E♭–G

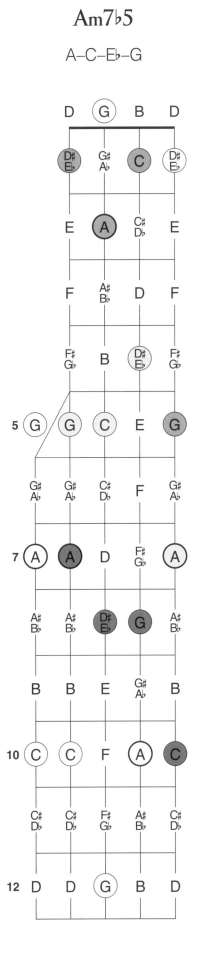

A♯/B♭m7♭5

A♯–C♯–E–G♯/B♭–D♭–F♭–A♭

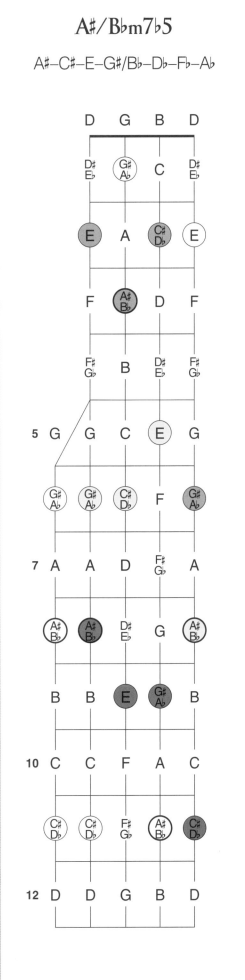

Bm7♭5

B–D–F–A

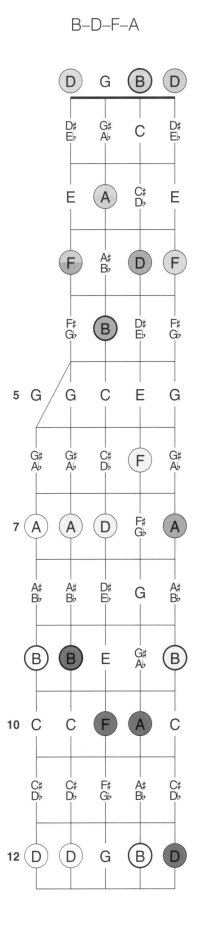

C°7

C–E♭–G♭–B♭♭

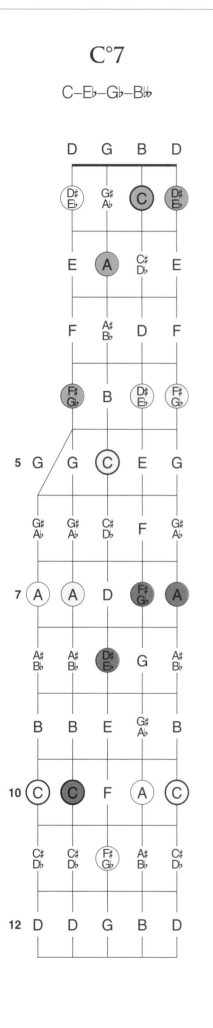

C#°7

C#–E–G–B♭

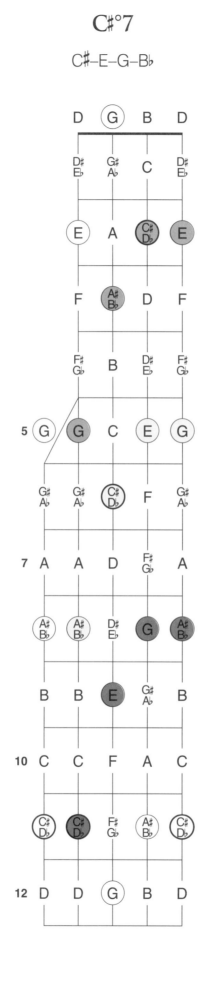

D°7

D–F–A♭–C♭

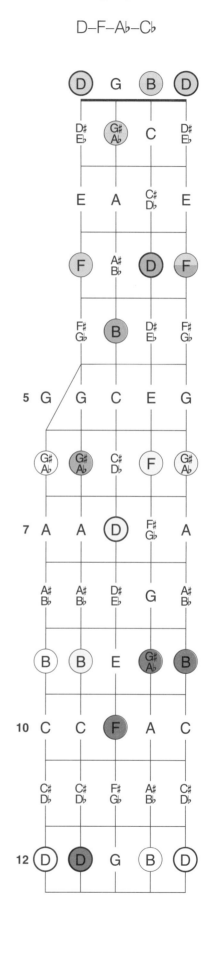

D#°7

D#–F#–A–C

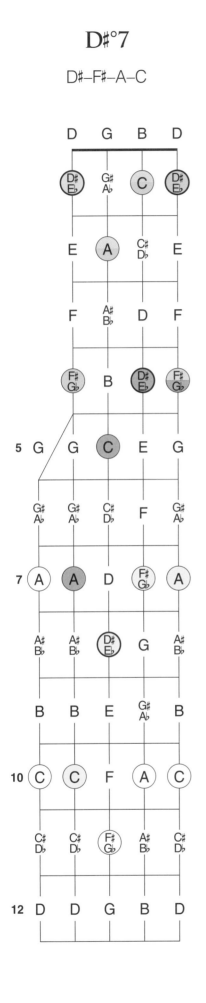

E°7

E–G–B♭–D♭

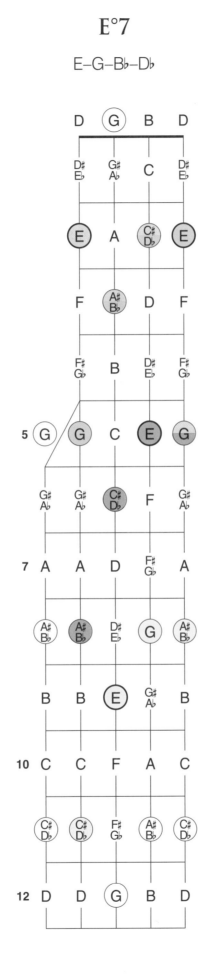

F°7

F–A♭–C♭–E♭♭

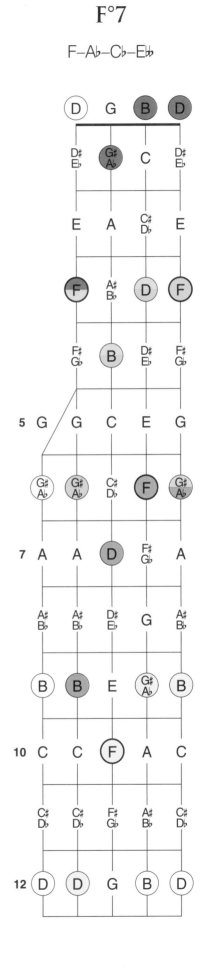

F#°7

F#–A–C–Eb

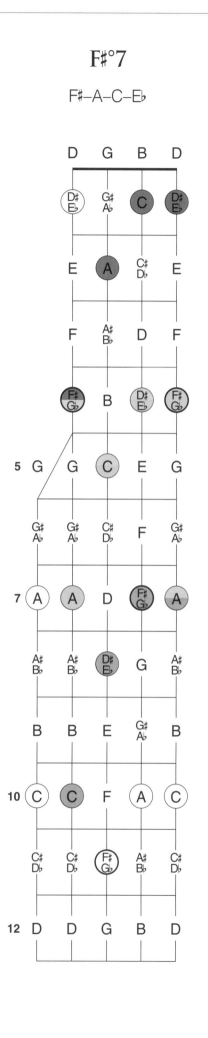

G°7

G–Bb–Db–Fb

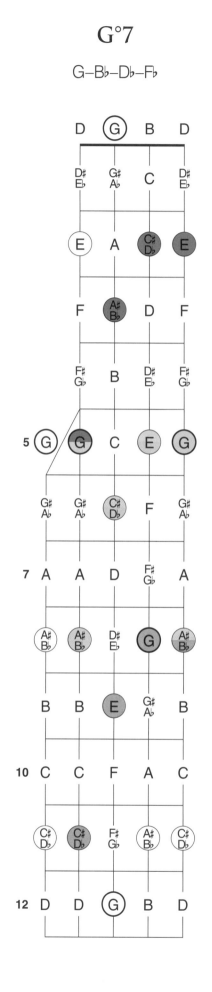

G#°7

G#–B–D–F

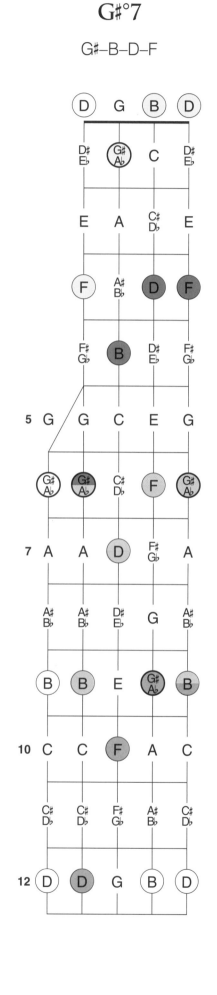

A°7

A–C–E♭–G♭

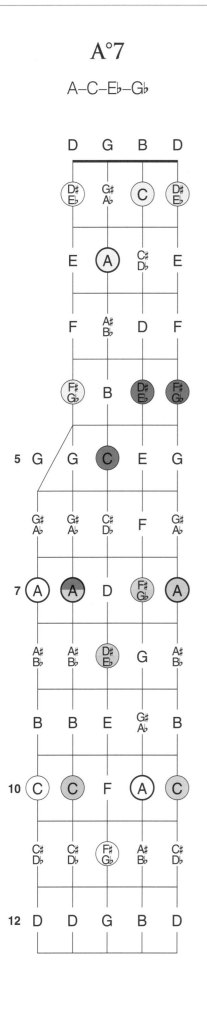

A♯/B♭°7

A♯–C♯–E–G/B♭–D♭–F♭–A♭♭

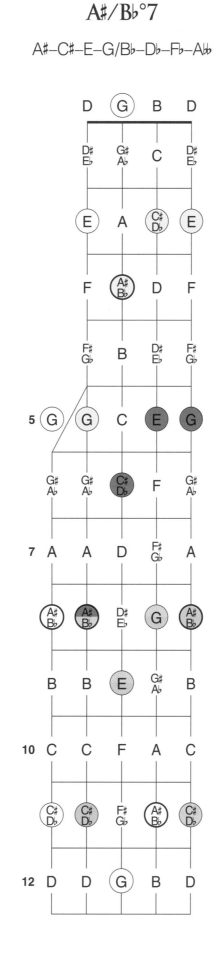

B°7

B–D–F–A♭

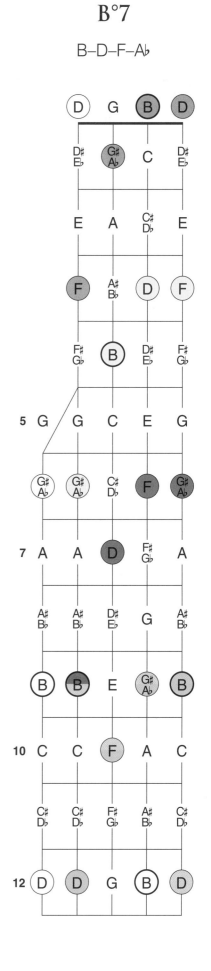

Hal Leonard Banjo Play-Along Series

HAL•LEONARD® BANJO PLAY-ALONG

AUDIO ACCESS INCLUDED

*The Banjo Play-Along Series will help you play your favorite songs quickly and easily with incredible backing tracks to help you sound like a bona fide pro! Just follow the banjo tab, listen to the demo track on the CD or online audio to hear how the banjo should sound, and then play along with the separate backing tracks. The CD is playable on any CD player and also is enhanced so Mac and PC users can adjust the recording to any tempo without changing the pitch! Books with online audio also include **PLAYBACK+** options such as looping and tempo adjustments. Each Banjo Play-Along pack features eight cream of the crop songs.*

INCLUDES TAB

1. BLUEGRASS
Ashland Breakdown • Deputy Dalton • Dixie Breakdown • Hickory Hollow • I Wish You Knew • I Wonder Where You Are Tonight • Love and Wealth • Salt Creek.
00102585 Book/CD Pack.........................$14.99

2. COUNTRY
East Bound and Down • Flowers on the Wall • Gentle on My Mind • Highway 40 Blues • If You've Got the Money (I've Got the Time) • Just Because • Take It Easy • You Are My Sunshine.
00105278 Book/CD Pack.........................$14.99

3. FOLK/ROCK HITS
Ain't It Enough • The Cave • Forget the Flowers • Ho Hey • Little Lion Man • Live and Die • Switzerland • Wagon Wheel.
00119867 Book/CD Pack.........................$14.99

4. OLD-TIME CHRISTMAS
Away in a Manger • Hark! the Herald Angels Sing • Jingle Bells • Joy to the World • O Holy Night • O Little Town of Bethlehem • Silent Night • We Wish You a Merry Christmas.
00119889 Book/CD Pack.........................$14.99

5. PETE SEEGER
Blue Skies • Get up and Go • If I Had a Hammer (The Hammer Song) • Kisses Sweeter Than Wine • Mbube (Wimoweh) • Sailing Down My Golden River • Turn! Turn! Turn! (To Everything There Is a Season) • We Shall Overcome.
00129699 Book/CD Pack.........................$17.99

6. SONGS FOR BEGINNERS
Bill Cheatham • Black Mountain Rag • Cripple Creek • Grandfather's Clock • John Hardy • Nine Pound Hammer • Old Joe Clark • Will the Circle Be Unbroken.
00139751 Book/CD Pack.........................$14.99

7. BLUEGRASS GOSPEL
Cryin' Holy unto the Lord • How Great Thou Art • I Saw the Light • I'll Fly Away • I'll Have a New Life • Man in the Middle • Turn Your Radio On • Wicked Path of Sin.
00147594 Book/Online Audio $14.99

8. CELTIC BLUEGRASS
Billy in the Low Ground • Cluck Old Hen • Devil's Dream • Fisher's Hornpipe • Little Maggie • Over the Waterfall • The Red Haired Boy • Soldier's Joy.
00160077 Book/Online Audio $14.99

www.halleonard.com